Like

Download your free printable Legit Work-at-Home Jobs Productivity Checklist on my website:

www.AshleyEmmaAuthor.com/fearlessauthorebook

Download free printable checklists at www.AshleyEmmaAuthor.com!

Legit Work-at-Home Jobs

A Quickstart Guide to 22+ Jobs and Business Ideas with Links to Help You Get Started

Ashley Emma

Check out my author Facebook page to see rare photos from when I lived with the Amish in Unity, Maine.

Copyright © 2016 by Ashley Emma

All rights reserved. No part of this book may be reproduced in any form or by any electronic or mechanical means, including information storage and retrieval systems, without the express written consent of the publisher, except by a reviewer, who may quote brief passages in a review.

Search for Ashley Emma on Amazon

Coming soon:

Table of Contents

LIKE FREE EBOOKS? 1

TABLE OF CONTENTS 7

INTRODUCTION 10

PART ONE: WORK-AT-HOME FAILURES, FLOPS, AND SUCCESSES 12

HOW TO SPOT A WORK-AT-HOME SCAM 12

WORK-AT-HOME JOBS THAT DID NOT WORK OUT WELL FOR ME 13

LEGIT WORK-AT-HOME JOBS FOR COMPANIES 15

ONLINE CLASSES AND COURSES ON STARTING YOUR OWN BUSINESS 20

FREELANCE WRITING AND VIRTUAL ASSISTANT WORK 21

PROOFREADING, SCOPING, AND EDITING 25

PROOFREADING 25

EDITING 30

SELLING ON AMAZON, SOCIAL MEDIA MANAGEMENT, DIRECT SALES, BLOGGING, WRITING BOOKS, GHOSTWRITING FOR CLIENTS, AND PUBLISHING BOOKS FOR CLIENTS 32

SELLING ON AMAZON 32

SOCIAL MEDIA MANAGEMENT 33

DIRECT SALES 35

BLOGGING 37

WRITING BOOKS (MY FAVORITE) 39

GHOSTWRITING FOR CLIENTS 45

PUBLISHING BOOKS FOR CLIENTS 47

STARTING YOUR OWN SALON AND DOING WEDDING SERVICES	54
MY AT-HOME SALON BUSINESS	54
HOW TO SELL HOMEMADE GREETING CARDS	68
TIPS AND TRICKS FOR SUCCEEDING IN ONLINE TUTORING	70
TEACH CLASSES ONLINE	72
PART TWO: GETTING ORGANIZED WHILE WORKING AT HOME	74
ORGANIZE YOUR HOME OFFICE	74
SETTING UP YOUR BUSINESS PROPERLY	78
ASHLEY'S LEGIT WORK-AT-HOME JOBS PRODUCTIVITY CHECKLIST:	81
WORK AT HOME JOBS LINKS LIST	86
BONUS SECTION: REAL STORIES FROM WORK-AT-HOME PROFESSIONALS	96
KEVIN'S STORY: WORKING FROM HOME CAN STILL BE A CALLING	99
MARIA'S STORY	102
RUSSEL'S STORY	104
ABOUT THE AUTHOR	108
LOOKING FOR SOMETHING NEW TO READ? CHECK OUT MY OTHER BOOKS!	110
HAVE YOU ALWAYS DREAMED OF BECOMING AN AUTHOR?	113
AN EXCERPT FROM *FEARLESS AUTHOR*: PREPARE, PUBLISH, AND LAUNCH YOUR OWN EBOOK	119

Legit Work-at-Home Jobs

A Quickstart Guide to 22+ Jobs and Business Ideas with Links to Help You Get Started

Introduction

So you want to make money from home? You've come to the right place.

I love working at home! I would never be able to go back to working for someone else. If you have children, you can stay home with your kids and have more time for your family. That is my favorite part of working at home. I don't have to send my children to daycare and I plan on homeschooling them when they are older while continuing to work.

One of the biggest benefits to a work-at-home gig is that you can work from anywhere you want. No fighting traffic, you can work in your pajamas if you want to (though experts don't recommend it), and you can set your own hours.

When you work for yourself, you're building your own empire, not someone else's.

You can work from a corner of your dining table, your couch, the library, your parents' house, Starbucks, the beach, a sunny backyard deck, or your home office.

Even if you are a teenager or retired, you can still make money at home or start your own business.

However, working from home is not always as easy as it sounds. Working at home doesn't mean you get to watch TV all day. It's real work, just like a regular job, but with more flexibility. Sometimes it can be even more work, but the reward is also greater. You are your own boss, but that also means you have no one to hold you accountable. It's also important to keep your work separate from your personal life, and I'll give you my tips on how to do that.

Fortunately, you have this guide which will help you avoid all the pitfalls I made when I first started working at home so your work-at-home journey can be as smooth as possible.

It took me a long time to find the perfect work-at-home job for me and I lost time and money in the process. With this book, you can find your perfect work-at-home job much sooner.

I wrote this no fluff, straight-to-the-point quick-start guide that shares all the work-at-home adventures and flops that I and other people I know have tried, along with our success stories.

This book is made of three parts. In Part 1, I will show you several jobs you can do from home and how to get started. Some of them you can start very quickly.

In Part 2, you will learn how to organize your home office, set up your business properly, and stay on task with Ashley's Work-at-Home Productivity Checklist.

In the bonus section, I share stories from some of my work-at-home friends who have started a successful business from home. These stories are about their struggles, successes, and tips on how you can get started doing these jobs as well.

I hope that you will learn from my mistakes as well as my successes.

I have worked at home for several years in my in-home hair salon and then as an author, writing and publishing my own books and now my clients' books. I also have proofread transcripts for court reporters, all while raising my kids. I used to edit books full time and now I still do it occasionally. I would love to do more editing once the rest of my books are published. I have an awesome husband who fully supports my dreams.

My most profitable and lucrative business has been publishing my own books along with running my publishing company. Through my publishing company, I publish books for my clients (aspiring authors and entrepreneurs who want to build their business) and I make ten times more money doing this than anything else I've ever done in my life.

It took a lot of trial and error to find the work-at-home business that was right for me. My goal in writing this book is to show you the many options you have available to you.

I'm glad that all of the time I spent trying out different work-at-home jobs didn't go to waste. Now I am using what I learned to help you work at home too.

You CAN work at home without a college degree. Read on to find out how.

When I got married two years ago, I started to look for an online job so I could make extra money. I was already working in the salon in my mom's house (it's now in my house). Back then I didn't have many clients so I wasn't making much money. I tried out so many different work-at-home jobs, and some of them were what I would consider to be shady or scams. Be careful—there are scams much worse than the ones I encountered. I will teach you how to spot them and avoid them.

Scammers love to prey on people who are desperate for an online job.

In this short eBook I will review some helpful classes that I took, some online jobs that were profitable for me, some that are good but weren't a good fit for me, and some that I do not recommend at all.

Part One: Work-At-Home Failures, Flops, and Successes

How To Spot A Work-At-Home Scam

There are thousands of work-at-home gigs out there. Some are legit, many are scams. Here is my simple checklist to help you evaluate whether an opportunity is a scam or not:

1. Never pay money to work from home. I am not against paying for an online course to help you work for yourself (as you will see in another section) or investing money into your own business. There are exceptions, but generally you should not have to pay money to work for someone else.

2. If it sounds too good to be true, it probably is. Use common sense when evaluating income claims for a potential work-from-home job. For example, if a company is promising you a ridiculously high amount of pay for minimal work, run away.

3. Do your homework. Always do your due diligence on any company you are considering working for. Google the company to see if there are any complaints about them. Check them out on the Better Business Bureau website or Glass Door (https://www.glassdoor.com/index.htm). If you see complaints, don't ignore them. Keep looking for a reputable company. They are out there.

4. Join work-from-home forums and Facebook groups that don't allow promotional material and are strictly for supporting each other. Just make sure the group is monitored by the administrator and doesn't have scammers lurking around, trying to recruit people.

It is great to make friends online with like-minded people who also share your passion to work for themselves. There are thousands of online communities out there where you can ask others who aspire to work from home about a company that you are interested in. If you are a mom, www.wahm.com has a great forum for work-at-home moms where you can find job leads and ask other WAHMs (work-at-home moms) about their experience with a company.

Work-At-Home Jobs That Did Not Work Out Well For Me

I do not recommend these two jobs, especially for work-at-home beginners.

It's up to you if you want to try them, but there are many others I recommend instead of these. Whatever you do, use caution.

AmeriPlan

AmeriPlan is a real work-at-home job. However, two of the reasons it didn't work for me were: I hate bugging friends and family to sign up for things, and AmeriPlan is basically unheard of where I live, which made it difficult to build my network. I did not like this experience because:

1. They charge money upfront just to work for them. You don't even get any sort of physical product out of it. I had to pay $50 for a membership to work for them when I signed up, then pay $17 a month for "leads."

2. I called to cancel my membership once I realized I couldn't sell AmeriPlan to anyone I knew here in the Northeast. About a year and a half later, I got a new debit card, and AmeriPlan contacted me for my card information. Back then, I wasn't smart enough to keep an eye on charges coming out of my bank account. Since then, I have learned my lesson. For a year and a half they charged me $17 a month for a service I thought I had canceled. The fees were $300 overall. Since we were newlyweds already low on money, I was distraught, realizing how much money had been lost.

This job was definitely not for me. But if you have good selling and networking sales and live in the area where their service is sold, this job might work for you.

Instant Rewards

Instant Rewards is another work-at-home online job I got into that I didn't like. This is a job that involves recruiting others to do the same job as you, which is to recruit more people. There were lots of things you had to pay for in order to start. That alone seemed fishy to me.

It might not have been a scam; I didn't stick with it long enough to find out, since I quickly realized I wasn't interested in trying to get people to sign up for their program.

The reason why I really didn't like it was because you had to try some "free" trials to get in. In one of the free trials I did, I had to order a sample "free" skin product (I never opened it), then send it back before a certain date. I sent it back on time, unopened, following all the rules, and they still charged me almost $100 for the product. Again, I was dismayed that I had lost more money. I should have seen the red flags, but at the time I was young and naïve. I don't recommend this company.

Basically, any online job that asks for money up front is probably a scam (this does not count online courses). Also, be wary of jobs that offer a ton of pay for minimal work.

Legit Work-At-Home Jobs For Companies

If you don't have the time or motivation to start your own business and you need cash fast, working at home for a company might be the way to go for you. There are a lot of pros and cons regarding working for yourself and working for a company. If you work for a company, you get a paycheck regularly and are usually paid hourly or per job. When you work for yourself, you can have busy months and some months with hardly any work at all, depending on what type of work you choose and how experienced you are. You may have work expenses when you work for yourself. However, when you think about the money you save on lunches, work clothing, and transportation, it is usually worth it.

Some people just want the security of working for a company rather than taking a risk and starting their own business, and that's totally fine. I've started a lot of businesses, and some took years to build and some took off in only a few weeks. For example, it took me a few years to build up a steady clientele for my in-home salon because I live in the country. However, my publishing company took only a few weeks to bring in thousands of dollars (more on this later).

Below are some jobs I tried for reputable companies I recommend. I chose to pursue my writing and publishing career, so I didn't have time to continue with these companies.

I'm glad I found these companies while I was searching for an online job so I can now share them with you.

For your convenience, I have added some information from each website.

Notice: The information for the companies below may change in the future so make sure you check their websites before applying.

Leap Force

http://www.leapforce.com

I actually never worked for Leap Force because they were not hiring at the time I looked into it. Leap Force employees are search engine evaluators. If you can get in, there is no startup fee, and they pay a good hourly wage (last I heard it was $15 an hour). You have to take an examination to qualify which I did not get the chance to take. This company is international so you can work from anywhere in the world.

Leapforce says on their site: "Leapforce is experiencing unprecedented demand and growth for qualified home-based independent agents. We are looking for highly educated individuals for an from home opportunity. Applicants must be self-motivated and Internet savvy. This ty to evaluate and improve search engine results for some of the world's largest engine companies. After you have completely read the requirements of becoming a LeapForce At Home Independent agent available here and have read the frequently asked questions about becoming an agent available here, please select from the following available opportunities."

Update: Since I wrote this section, Appen has acquired Leap Force.

Appen

https://join.appen.com/

Appen employs social media evaluators. I was very interested in working in this position, but you must work at least four hours a day to maintain the position. That just didn't work with my schedule. According to Appen's website, consultants must complete a one-week trial period. You must be comfortable with social media, proficient at writing in English, and able to follow directions well. Their website also lists other opportunities that seem like they are worth checking out.

Appen's website says: "Appen helps leading companies expand into new global markets. We create a better experience for customers by improving search engines, social media platforms, eCommerce sites and more. With a crowd of over 400,000 flexible people in over 130 countries working in more than 180 languages and dialects, we help our clients ramp up their teams so they can respond to ever-changing customer needs. Appen offers work from home opportunities for exciting, flexible, short-term projects as well as full-time corporate opportunities. We are proud to be named as one of the Top 100 Companies Offering Flexible Jobs in 2014, 2015, 2016 and 2017, by FlexJobs."

WritersDomain

http://www.writersdomain.net

You don't need an English degree to work for them, but you do need to submit a writing sample. They ask you to write a sample article on a certain subject and submit it. At the time I was looking into applying, they weren't hiring, so I didn't end up working for them. You can get paid $15 to $38 an article. The thing is, you can spend a lot of time on an article for them if you get hired, but if it is not approved, you don't get paid for it.

Their website says: "At WritersDomain, you get paid to do what you love! We match top writing talent from around the world with thousands of assignments every month from our small business clients. The work our writers do helps our clients succeed online. Founded in May, 2011, WritersDomain is a branch of the online marketing company Boostability. We now have over 450 active writers around the world who complete work for our clients in the United States, Canada, Germany, the Netherlands, and even Australia. Our platform operates on a first-come, first-served basis, so if there's work available, you can write as much as you want."

Rev

https://www.rev.com/freelancers/captions

Rev is a very reputable closed captioning company that captions video material for the hearing impaired. They also transcribe recordings. I know authors who record themselves talking and have the recordings transcribed by Rev to create a written manuscript.

You have to take a lengthy test to be accepted. It took me several hours, but I did get in. You probably could make pretty good money doing this, but I was too slow to make much from it. Additionally, I was writing a book at the time, so I gave up. I could always go back to it, since there is no minimum requirement of work you have to complete monthly.

You get to choose any project you want, and when the company has a lot of work to get done, they offer higher pay. At the time of writing this, you can earn $0.50 to $0.75 per AUDIO minute, which means that you get paid depending on how long the video is, not how many minutes it takes you. But if you do it enough, you would probably get faster and be able to earn more. You type what you hear, and there are a few tricky rules, but once I got the hang of it, it was kind of fun.

It took me about a half hour to transcribe six minutes of audio, so that would amount to about $9 an hour. However, everyone will go at different paces. But that's not a bad starting point, and of course you will get faster as you get more practice.

I was too busy to stick with it, but it could be the right job for you.

Want to make money while working on classic TV shows, modern movies, educational videos, and more?

Rev's website says: "Rev.com is the best place to find freelance work online. Our new captions service has a ton of content by top-tier video producers. We're looking to add captioners to our freelance Revver caption team. Apply, be accepted, and start earning in under 48 hours. Earn $0.40-$0.75 per video minute. Paid weekly, via PayPal. Average monthly earnings: $240. Top monthly earnings: $1570. Work from home. Work wherever you want. Everything is done online. Work flexible hours. Work as much or as little as you want, whenever you want. Choose freely. Choose which projects you want to work on. We have a wide variety available. Receive great support. Our fantastic support team resolves issues promptly. Get started easily. All you need is a computer, headset, broadband Internet, and strong English skills."

If you want a job with a short amount of training you can do from home, with no startup fee (except maybe buying a headset or laptop if you don't already have one), working for Rev could be it.

VIP Desk

https://vipdeskconnect.com/current-openings/

VIP Desk hires customer service agents who work from home full- or part-time. They only hire agents in the United States at the time of writing this, and they only hire in these states: AZ, CO, FL, GA, IL, IN, MD, NJ, NV, NY, OH, TX, UT, and VA. (This may change in the future.) You can make your own schedule, but you must work holidays and stick to the schedule you make. You must login on time.

Their website says: "We value our employees as much as our customers. We work with you every step of the way to ensure you have the right tools and training to succeed. Plus, working from home has many benefits! It is environmentally friendly (the farthest you have to travel is across your house) which means you save on gas, tolls and eliminate the stress of traveling. Also, by eliminating the commute, you get to spend more time with your family and friends! We're always on the lookout for talented individuals who are passionate about delivering exceptional customer service. We continually recruit and cultivate highly capable professionals from a wide variety of backgrounds to join our work-at-home virtual team in providing top notch customer service. We recognize that happy team members translate into positive customer experiences, which invariably results in satisfied clients. We provide a supportive and positive work environment, that's why we match our team members' talents and interests with the brands they serve. Are you passionate about delivering exceptional customer service? Are you motivated, self-disciplined, and ready to live the brand you serve? If so, feel free to search our open positions, but first, check out our core values. They are our DNA and central to how we do business."

Their website also says what their job requirements are, such as having a separate room for your home office, under the FAQ section which is under the Careers section.

Convergys

http://www.convergys.com

Convergys offers work-at-home call center positions all over the world. This is a job that requires you to be on the phone, and you get a lot of calls. That might not ideal if you have little kids at home unless you have someone to watch them while you work. But according to the website, they offer paid training, a variety of schedules, and full benefits. Pretty sweet!

Their website says: "We are looking for great people who have a passion for customer service. Instead of working in a traditional call center environment, our Convergys Work At Home program hires customer service agents who work directly from home. We have three basic types of work for home positions; all are required to provide customer service support. Some positions are more sales or technically focused. During the application process you will be asked to identify which of these positions most interests you. Your qualifications and experience will be reviewed as part of the evaluation process."

They also list these benefits of working for them on their site:

"How do you know if working at home with Convergys is right for you?

- You would like a full benefit package with medical, vision, and dental coverage.
- You would like to earn paid vacation.
- You would like to participate in a 401-K plan and be reimbursed for college tuition.
- You would like all your training and work to be virtual, working out of your own home office that you set up and design to your liking.
- You would like the confidence that comes from superior, quality training.
- You would like to be part of a team of professionals that has fun and actually enjoys working together."

Online Classes And Courses On Starting Your Own Business

Personally, I think starting your own business is the way to go. It might require a lot of work at the beginning, but once you get established, you will love not having to ask for days off. You are your own boss. How fantastic is that? It could start out as a side job until you get busy enough, then you could transition into full time.

I started my own businesses at home. I make my own schedule. I set my own prices. I work alone, and I wouldn't have it any other way. Honestly, I prefer to work alone. I like to work when I want, the way I want, without having to ask a boss for permission to do something. I also write books, obviously.

You may be wondering how in the world I learned how to do all of these things. I did teach myself a lot of what I know, but I love taking online courses. The Internet has opened an entire world of information on how to do anything you want to do. If you have a passion for something and want to learn how to do it, you can probably find an online course on that subject.

In this next section I will tell you about the online courses I took that helped me start my business and other work-at-home jobs I have enjoyed doing.

Please note: Some of the course or product links in this book are affiliate links, but I only recommend products or courses that I have personally tried and absolutely love. I would be raving about them anyway even if I weren't an affiliate because they have helped me so much, and I have done so. I decided to sign up for the affiliate programs after I had already written about them in this book. I want to be up front and honest with you about this.

The courses I have listed in this book are some of the best courses I've ever taken, and I've taken a lot of courses. They are absolutely worth the money. I love taking online courses and broadening my set of skills. Taking these courses helped me get to where I am today.

Keep reading if you're interested in finding out how you can take a course to help you launch your own online business!

Freelance Writing And Virtual Assistant Work

Gina Horkey's Classes

Gina Horkey is a wonderful person and well-known in the world of writing from home.

30 Days or Less to Freelance Writing Success

This class is super affordable and teaches you everything you need to know about how to start your own writing business (writing articles, blog posts, etc.). At the time of writing this, it is $147. It will probably keep going up in price because it's awesome. You do it at your own pace, and there are even checklists, quizzes, and an exam. If you like writing, this could be a great new way to start your new writing career. I highly recommend it.

For information on Gina Horkey's Freelance Writing online courses, just go to www.horkeyhandbook.com or use my affiliate links below:

30 Days or Less to Freelance Writing Success Course:

https://horkeyhandbook.com/30-days-new-freelance-writing-career/?sc_ref=RO7AGdsWbyYJMdKj

Free "How to Become a Freelance Writer" Blogpost:

https://horkeyhandbook.samcart.com/referral/how-to-become-a-paid-freelance-writer/RO7AGdsWbyYJMdKj

Not sure what writing niche to specialize in?

https://horkeyhandbook.samcart.com/referral/freelance-writing-niches/RO7AGdsWbyYJMdKj

Check out Gina's site:

www.horkeyhandbook.com

or

https://horkeyhandbook.samcart.com/referral/Homepage/RO7AGdsWbyYJMdKj

30 Days or Less to Virtual Assistant Success

Another growing field that is in high demand is virtual assistants. You can find a full-time gig for one client, or split your time between multiple clients. There are virtual assistant agencies that you register with that will bring job offers to you. An agency will typically take a cut of your profits, but you won't have to spend the time to find new clients.

There are several online classes such as Gina Horkey's class, (www.horkeyhandbook.com) that you can take to learn the skills you need to find clients and manage all aspects of your business. However, if you have some basic administrative skills, you can easily begin your VA career by securing that first client and moving on from there. I honestly signed up for this course mostly out of curiosity, and though I liked the course a lot, I decided to pursue writing instead. A virtual assistant could be a great at-home job for you if you are organized, persistent, and willing to offer a variety of services from checking someone's email to booking appointments for them. You can make $20-$100 an hour as a VA. Regardless of what you charge in the beginning, you can always increase your rates as you get busier and gain more experience. You can also charge a daily or weekly rate. At the time of writing this, this course is also $147.

You work for yourself, so you can charge whatever you want.

What kind of services do virtual assistants offer? The options are almost endless:

- Answer phone calls and emails
- Write articles and blog posts
- Manage a travel calendar
- Schedule clients
- Publish email newsletters
- Create PowerPoint presentations
- Provide customer service via chat
- Manage an online store
- Bookkeeping and payroll
- Generate reports
- Data entry
- Proofreading and editing
- Social media management
- Many, many other tasks

Easy Steps to Start Your Virtual Assistant Career

I spoke with my friend Nicole who gave me a few tips on how to start a virtual assistant business with little additional training or upfront investment. By following her tips, you could have your business running very quickly. I like how simple her approach is.

This is what she told me:

1. **Find your first client:** I got started in my VA business by simply applying to virtual assistant jobs online. I put together a strong resume by searching online for "virtual assistant resume samples" and getting ideas for how to best showcase my administrative experience. Don't copy a sample resume word-for-word, but use it for ideas. I had worked several office jobs in the past, so I highlighted all of the skills that I could bring to the table and sent off my resume.

   I applied to jobs on Craigslist and Upwork mostly, but I found my first job by applying to a position that I found on a message board for work-at-home moms. Starting with that one client, I tried to exceed her expectations on every task. She recommended me to her other entrepreneur friends, and the business grew from there.

2. **Offer to do small, one-time jobs to prove yourself:** Many clients will ask you to perform smaller tasks before hiring you as their VA. When you get these offers, over deliver on the task so that you can give your client a taste of what it would be like to work with you regularly. Once you complete a task, you have the opportunity to upsell. Let the client know about additional ways that you can help them in their business. Sell the benefits of securing you as a regular remote assistant.

3. **Consistently apply for new jobs and remind current clients that you love referrals:** Be on the lookout for new VA jobs and keep your resume circulating. Join social media groups for virtual assistants and make friends. I've had busy VA friends refer me to clients that they were unable to take on. You can also learn a ton of tips from other successful VAs on things like how to deal with difficult clients or how to handle your bookkeeping.

4. **Treat it like a business:** Make sure that you project a professional image in all of your emails and on social media. Set up a separate bank account for your VA business and keep good records of all of your income and expenses to avoid headaches at tax time. Never stop learning and growing in your field. Your clients will take notice.

For information on Gina Horkey's Virtual Assistant online courses, just go to www.horkeyhandbook.com or use my affiliate links below:

Gina Horkey's 30 Days or Less to Virtual Assistant Success Course:

https://horkeyhandbook.samcart.com/referral/30-Days-or-Less-to-Virtual-Assistant-Success-Sales-Page/RO7AGdsWbyYJMdKj

Free "How to Become a Virtual Assistant" Blogpost:

https://horkeyhandbook.samcart.com/referral/how-to-become-a-virtual-assistant/RO7AGdsWbyYJMdKj

Not sure what services to offer as a new Virtual Assistant? Check out this helpful link:

https://horkeyhandbook.samcart.com/referral/va-services-list/RO7AGdsWbyYJMdKj

Check out Gina's site:

www.horkeyhandbook.com
(https://horkeyhandbook.samcart.com/referral/shop/RO7AGdsWbyYJMdKj)

Success Stories:

https://horkeyhandbook.samcart.com/referral/sss/RO7AGdsWbyYJMdKj

Virtual Assistant finder:

https://horkeyhandbook.samcart.com/referral/2aIdgwUw/RO7AGdsWbyYJMdKj

Proofreading, Scoping, And Editing

Proofreading

As I discussed in the Online Classes section, I took a class on legal transcript proofreading. Now Caitlin also offers a course on General Proofreading.

If you think you'd be interested in proofreading professionally, this section is for you.

If you are good with grammar, like to read, and know how to pay attention to detail, proofreading might be a good business for you to look into. Freelance proofreaders can make good money spotting errors in legal transcripts, articles, blog posts, sales materials, websites, books, and just about any kind of document you can think of.

Keep in mind that legal transcript proofreading is different than general proofreading because the rules are different. So while you may like one, you might not like the other. Or you might like both. Read on to see which one(s) you might like.

Caitlin Pyle's Proofreading Courses

Caitlin Pyle has established herself as an expert in the world of proofreading, starting the first online course that teaches people how to proofread legal transcripts before she turned thirty.

This section is about my experience with one of her courses in particular, her legal transcript proofreading course called *Proofread Anywhere*.

I absolutely loved her legal transcript proofread course, but let me tell you like it is; it is NOT quick and easy. First of all, you're going to have to invest a good amount of money in this class.

When I joined *Proofread Anywhere* in winter 2015, I paid a very low price because it was still new. Now it costs over $1,000 for the basic legal proofreading package.

However, if you want to make a career out of transcript proofreading, this course is absolutely worth the money. The Facebook group support alone is worth the price of the training.

Caitlin has added a lot more to the course material, and the popularity of this class has exploded. Check out her website for awesome testimonials. You can make good money proofreading legal transcripts because there is plenty of work out there. Plus, court reporters often stick with you and become regular clients, so you can stay busy enough with a few of them rather than constantly trying to find work.

The class is worth the price if you are sure it is a good fit for you. Think about the money people spend on college degrees that they sometimes don't end up using. This class takes 2-4 months to complete on average. It took me 6 months because I took a few breaks from it to write a book and go on maternity leave. If you are determined, this could be a great choice for you.

I did finish the course, and I proofread legal transcripts part-time for about six months. When my books began to really take off, I stopped proofreading to focus on writing and publishing more books, which is my true passion. However, I really did enjoy proofreading transcripts just as I enjoyed editing books, and I had some great clients. I plan on doing it again when my kids are older, and I have several books published.

You must have a good eye for grammatical errors. When I read articles or books, errors usually "pop off the page" at me.

If this doesn't happen to you, let me save you a lot of trouble by telling you that it won't be a good fit for you. And Caitlin will tell you the same thing. She is super honest.

If you love English, spelling, reading, and punctuation, go for it. I hope you like these topics, because you will have to proofread over 3,000 practice pages. Yes, 3,000.

If you decide this course is for you, you might want to invest in an iPad. I bought the basic iPad Mini and proofread on that because it is the quickest, most effective way to proofread. There's an excellent app you can proofread on, but you need the iPad to use it. Plus, I bring it with me everywhere and proofread on the go.

You do have to pass a few tests with a score of 90 or above to make it to the next module, so you must study hard to succeed. Most graduates make over $1500 in their first two months of work after graduating.

Caitlin posted her income report for 2014: She made over $7,000 in April 2014 alone proofreading part-time and made $40,000 a year working 20-25 hours a week. Imagine what you could make full-time. You won't become a millionaire, but it sounds pretty good to me if you can work on your couch while bringing in some steady dough.

Caitlin has been an inspiration to me. She has a great blog and is very quick to answer any questions. Since her job can be done anywhere, she moved from Florida to Ecuador.

If proofreading legal transcripts doesn't sound fun to you, you may be interested in her General Proofreading Course. Or, book editing or scoping may be more your style (more info on that later.)

Either way, here are a few tips to help you get started in freelance proofreading:

1. Get educated. Unless you have a degree in English or some experience proofreading, you'll

want to brush up on your grammar school studies. You can take classes online or at a local community college.

2. Stay current on the latest grammar rules. English grammar has a lot of rules that are widely debated among experts and writers. Keep learning by following good grammar blogs like Grammar Girl: www.quickanddirtytips.com/grammar-girl.

3. Build your portfolio. If you have no experience proofreading, there are some simple ways to start building your portfolio. Join a freelance website like www.fiverr.com and offer your services for a very low rate. When bidding for a job you can say something like, "Hello, I am a freelance proofreader who is new to (insert website name), and I am offering a low introductory rate for new clients in order to gain some reviews here." Do five very cheap jobs and over-deliver on each job. After this, you will have a great portfolio, five amazing reviews, and some valuable experience in your new business. Raise your rates to something you would be happy to make.

4. In the beginning, double the length of time you say you will have something done. For example, when one is just starting, they can say they will be done with a project in 15 days. In your mind, you know it'll probably be done in 7 days, but it's better to tell the client the latter. Then, if you do get done in 7 days, the client will be very happy and give you an even a better review.

5. Offer your services for free on a writer's forum. This is a great way to break into proofreading books. Simply write a post stating you are a freelance proofreader and that you would like to add a few books to your resume, but make sure you ask for permission first from the person in charge of the site. Offer to proofread 30 pages or so for free in exchange for an honest testimonial. If you do a great job, you might find your first paying client this way. Either way, you can add this job to your resume and put their testimonials on your website. Again, make sure you ask permission first so you don't get in trouble. Don't ask for positive or good testimonials. Only ask for honest testimonials.

6. Create a simple website that tells potential customers about you and your services. Include your portfolio. If you have no experience with websites, hire someone to create one for you online. Your website doesn't have to be fancy. A simple page about your services, rates, and background is enough to get started.

I recommend:

http://wixstats.com/?a=16616&c=2252&s1=

https://wordpress.com/

Get the word out. Tell everyone you know about your new business. Email friends and family and let them know what you are doing. Send messages to your friends on social media letting them know what you are doing. Get business cards made and hand one to everyone you meet. You never know who may need your services.

These are only a few ideas to get you started. A good book or class on starting a general proofreading business will give you step-by-step instructions on how to build your business. *The Editor's Companion* by Steve Dunham and *McGraw-Hill's Proofreading Handbook* by Laura Anderson are two must-have books. You also want to have a copy of the *Chicago Manual of Style* handy.

For legal transcript proofreading only, check out Margie Wakeman Wells' resources at www.margieholdscourt.com.

More info on Proofread Anywhere:

http://www.businessinsider.com/caitlin-pyle-proofread-anywhere-2015-8

https://proofreadanywhere.com/work-at-home-job-ideas-for-detail-oriented-people/

And for fun, check out this article I wrote with Caitlin: https://proofreadanywhere.com/3-reasons-you-should-consider-self-publishing-a-book-and-how-to-get-started/

You can also try out a free mini-course here:

https://caitlinpyle.com/optin

The Proofread Anywhere Legal Transcript Course:

https://caitlinpyle.com/pa

Caitlin recently opened a new class called General Proofreading: Theory and Practice. While I haven't taken this class personally, I would highly recommend any class taught by Caitlyn Pyle. She offers a free 45-minute seminar to help prospective students determine whether or not a career in proofreading is right for them.

Here is the link:

https://learn.proofreadanywhere.com/registergptpfb?affiliate_id=690241

Editing

Scoping (Editing Court Transcripts)

Scope School

Another course using a love of grammar and punctuation is Linda Evenson's Internet Scope School. Scoping is editing court transcripts using audio files. The average scopist earns anywhere from $30,000 to $50,000 a year from home. Like legal transcript proofreaders, scopists often receive regular work from a small group of court reporters.

The tuition includes lifetime access to the course, so you can take it at your own pace. You can also try out a free mini-course to learn more about scoping by using the link below:

https://scopeschool.com/ashleyemma/1

Editing Books

The Christian PEN

https://thechristianpen.com/

Ever wanted to edit books? I'd recommend starting here.

And no, you do not need a degree to edit books and you can make very good money.

I love this organization. It is run by some great people. I took *Establishing Your Freelance Business* by Kathy Ide (a fantastic editor who has worked on some of my writing). She's a great teacher and taught us how to start an editing business from home. She never took a college class and makes $60 an hour editing books.

The Christian PEN is constantly offering a rotation of different classes on writing and editing. If you become a member, you get a discount. They have an email group that supports each other by asking and answering questions.

They offer valuable information and they send you a spiffy certificate of completion after you finish a course to hang in your office. Score!

When you are ready to look for editing work, check out The Christian Editor Connection. This website connects editors to authors, agents, and publishers. This matching service is free for authors, agents, and publishers. Editors pay a $50 annual membership fee to receive job leads. It's well worth it, in my opinion.

Here is the link: https://christianeditor.com/editors/

Here is the link to their school The Pen Institute: https://peninstitue.com

Selling on Amazon, Social Media Management, Direct Sales, Blogging, Writing Books, Ghostwriting for Clients, and Publishing Books for Clients

Selling on Amazon

Amazon FBA and The Selling Family

I haven't had any personal experience with Amazon FBA, but my friend Nicole has told me about her experience with it and this great course from The Selling Family. There are a lot of people making good money with Amazon FBA, so I wanted to include a short section on it for you.

For those of you that are unfamiliar with Amazon FBA, or Fulfillment by Amazon, anyone with a little startup capital and some know-how can sell products utilizing Amazon's huge marketplace. Through the FBA program, you can store your products in Amazon's warehouses, and when you receive a sale, Amazon packs and ships the order to your customer for you. Amazon of course charges fees for the ability to utilize their warehouses, as well as packing and shipping services; however, selling your products on Amazon's global marketplace allows you to reach customers that you probably couldn't have reached on your own.

How do you find products to sell on Amazon? Many FBA sellers, like Nicole, use retail arbitrage to find products. This means that she scours the clearance racks, thrift stores, eBay, and even Amazon itself for great deals on products that she can sell for a profit on Amazon. Without going into a lot of detail on how to find the right products, Nicole recommends The Selling Family blog (https://thesellingfamily.com) and their online courses.

According to Nicole, The Selling Family blog offers a great overview on Amazon FBA and retail arbitrage, and their Amazon Bootcamp class taught her everything she needed to know about how to get started. Check out the blog if this sounds like something you want to learn more about.

Social Media Management

By Ashley Emma and Nicole Cruz

If you can't get through the day without scrolling through your newsfeed or letting everyone on Instagram know what you're up to, social media management might be the perfect business idea for you. Many business owners are either clueless about how to maintain an effective social media presence or don't have the time. These entrepreneurs will gladly pay you to handle all of their social media for them.

Some freelance social media professionals charge their clients as much as $1,000 to $3,000 a month. Others charge $20-$50 or more per hour. How much you charge will be based upon your experience and what kind of results you are promising your clients. In most freelance businesses, clients will pay large rates for the results that they seek. If you can show a business owner that you can give them more engagement on their social media, more prospects, or more sales, they will gladly pay you whatever rate you ask for.

Learning the Business

While running social media pages is different than posting to your personal accounts, it is not a hard business to learn if you already have some basic knowledge of how social media works. There are several online classes and books that will show you how to create and maintain a powerful social media presence for businesses. A quick Google search will give you many options which are always changing. Do your research and go with the class that has the best reviews. There is a ton of free information online as well. If you don't have the money to invest in a class, this can give you a great start.

Build Your Social Media Presence

Once you have the knowledge, it's time to establish your own professional social media presence. When you are just starting out, this will be the only reference point that you will have to show potential clients, so spend some serious time on your own social media accounts. Show off what you can do for your clients, and start building your online network. Engage with your followers regularly, and post valuable information that shows your expertise.

Find Your First Client

Your next order of business is to find that first client. A good online class will give you several ideas on how to do this. One of the best ways to get started in any business is to use your network. Reach out to everyone you know, and let them know what you are doing. Tell them that you just completed a class on how to manage social media and you are offering a steep discount for first-time clients. You may want to offer your services for free for the first month or barter. Work hard to exceed your customers' expectations, and you will build a reputation that will bring you new clients by word of mouth.

Once you have a few clients under your belt, raise your rates and continue to learn more about your industry so that you can offer your clients a service that they will want to pay top dollar for.

A wonderful woman named Liz Benny also teaches a course called Social Monkey Business on how to become a 6-figure social media manager. I am taking her Kapow Course which teaches how to create online courses, and Liz is the real deal. She is honest, genuine, and really quite hilarious. I would recommend any of her trainings. She really cares about her students and personally answers questions in her Facebook groups. I've never seen a course creator be so involved in their students' success. She really wants you to succeed.

"Being a Social Media Manager is not just about posting stuff on a client's Facebook page and hoping for the best. I want to show you exactly how it is that I've scaled my business so it's very profitable, but in a way that always provides value for my clients." -Liz Benny, founder of Jinga Social

She has a free webclass you can sign up for called "How To be a Successful, Highly Paid Social Media Manager": https://socialmonkeybusiness.com/special-webinar-event?affiliate_id=922937

Here are some more links to get you started as a social media manager:

http://socialmarketingwriting.com/complete-guide-successful-social-media-manager/

http://www.socialmediatoday.com/content/9-steps-starting-out-social-media-manager

Direct Sales

By Ashley Emma and Nicole Cruz

Companies like Avon, Thrive, Herbalife, and Amway have been around for a long time, and they offer opportunities for anyone who is willing to invest in a business to work as an independent distributor. These companies typically offer an extensive training program so that you can learn how to sell their products without any previous experience.

Do Your Research on Any Company

Some companies place you with a mentor who can help you get started. While there are many legitimate direct sales opportunities out there, be wary of any company that only teaches you how to recruit more people into the business and nothing else. Recruiting new representatives should only be part of the business, not your sole focus.

Direct Sales is Not a Job, It's a Business

I think that it is important to note here that I am not going against my own advice that you shouldn't pay to work for any company. Direct sales is an independent business, and any money you pay to the company is an investment in your business. Expenses such as inventory and training are all part of the cost of doing business.

There are so many direct sales business opportunities available now that I couldn't possibly cover all of them in this little section. The link below will show you the top 100 direct selling companies by annual revenue as of the printing of this book. Again, do your research on any company before you sign up. Be sure to read all of the fine print to be sure that you understand all of the policies and how the compensation plan works.

http://directsellingnews.com/index.php/view/dsn_announces_the_2017_global_100#.Wd-ORWhSzIU

The Money Making Mommy blog also came out with a handy directory of direct sales companies divided by interest. For example, if you want to sell essential oils, you can look under that section and the direct sales companies that offer essential oils. You can then compare your options and choose the right fit for you. It appears that this link is updated every year, so don't be thrown off by the date at the end of the link. Here it is:

https://www.moneymakingmommy.com/direct-sales-company-list-2011/

Go With Your Passion

The bottom line when choosing a direct sales company is to choose a company with a strong track record and products that you are passionate about. If you choose a great company with products that you are either not very interested in or embarrassed to tell people that you sell, you won't sell a thing. If you sell products that you love to use yourself and are happy to talk about with your close friends, as well as the stranger in the grocery line, chances are you'll do very well.

Blogging

By Ashley Emma and Nicole Cruz

Is blogging right for you?

You can make money blogging, but it requires a lot of work and time.

- You must love to write. Blogging experts differ on how often you need to blog in order to be successful. Some say that you need to blog every day, while others say you can have a thriving blog by posting only 1-2 awesome posts per week. Either way, you'll need to be committed to spending the time to research, write, edit, and rewrite a lot of content on a consistent basis.

- You must dedicate at least 2-4 hours a day on your blog. Some bloggers do it only as a hobby, which is great. But if you want to make some money off your blog, you need to be prepared to spend time writing and marketing your blog. The more money you want to make, the more you need to be working on getting your blog out there.

- You must be prepared to invest in your blog. You don't have to invest a ton of money in your blog at first, but you'll need to invest in a good webhosting plan, a domain name, a quality theme, and a good blogging class. (More on this below.)

How Can I Get Started?

Although blogging is not an easy way to make money, there has never been an easier time to start a blog. There are a ton of resources online that you can use to learn everything you need to know to start your blog. If you are willing to invest the time, money, and effort to learn what you need to know, blogging can be a very lucrative business for you.

If you are really strapped for cash, you can get started very easily by googling, "how to start a Wordpress blog," and you will find a wealth of information to get you started. You can join a webhosting service such as Bluehost (www.bluehost.com) or Hostgator (www.hostgator.com) and purchase your domain name for less than $100. Do an online search for promo codes for either company and you might find a good deal. If webhosts and domain names are like a foreign language to you, you'll probably want to join a class.

Which Blogging Classes and Resources Do You Recommend?

Check out Crystal Paine's website http://moneysavingmom.com/about for tips on how t⁻ money-making blog, or just to do it for fun. Crystal also has a lot of awesome tip⁻ money on groceries, how to set goals, and free email courses on making ⁻

home. I took her $10 course Makeover Your Mornings (told you I love online classes), and it was fabulous. There are also a lot of free resources on how to blog.

Tanya at www.blogelina.com has an easy-to-understand article on how to get your blog started in less than 10 minutes http://blogelina.com/how-to-start-your-own-profitable-blog. Her blog has tons of informative posts on blogging, and she offers a very inexpensive 4-week class that will teach you everything you need to know about starting and running a successful blog.

Jon Morrow has an excellent site called Smart Blogger that shows you how to make more money blogging: https://smartblogger.com/start-here/

Writing Books (My favorite)

Okay, this is definitely not for everyone, but I figured I would tell you about my writing journey and give you a few pointers. If you do this right, you could make money on the side writing books at home. If your books really take off, it could turn into a full-time income. It takes a while to get going, but once you set your books up and launch them, it gets easier as you go.

Let's be realistic. Notice I keep saying 'books' because the more you publish, the more you will make. You probably won't get rich from your first book. If you are passionate, have multiple books, and market them regularly, they can become several streams of income that build up. The more books you have, the more they sell each other. And if they do take off, then you can certainly make a full-time income from your books, but it won't happen overnight.

Let's compare the different forms of publishing.

Self-Publishing (my favorite method)

I could write a whole other book on this… And, I did. Here I will briefly cover self-publishing, but I cover it in much more detail in my bestselling book *Fearless Author: How to Prepare, Publish, and Launch Your Own eBook,* which you can find here: http://a.co/5IqzNDR

In it you will find a boatload of resources that will help you publish a successful eBook. I generated over $17,000 of client work with this book in its first month alone (I self-publish books for my clients or coach them through it).

I was 14 when I wrote my first full-length book, and 12 when I wrote my first novella *The Secret City*. I self-published my second book on Amazon.com when I was 16, and it took off from there. To be successful, you need to be willing to learn the KDP system, marketing, and other skills. The time and effort was worth it to me because I'm extremely passionate about writing and self-publishing.

If you think you have a passion for writing and marketing your own books, read on to learn more about how self-publishing works.

You keep all your royalties with self-publishing instead of splitting it with a publisher and agent. Also, you can publish books much more rapidly instead of waiting for an agent and publisher, which can take up to two years per book. I publish several books a year. You can hire ghostwriters too.

My author friend makes over five figures a month publishing several eBooks on Amazon a month, and she has over 150 published. Depending on the niche and how many you publish a month, you could do several series of short reads and quickly build a readership and following, and you could hire a ghostwriter to help you if you don't have the time to write them yourself or don't want to.

I made a few hundred dollars a year on my four eBooks when I was a teenager, but now that I know the secrets to making a book successful, my self-published books are much more successful. And I reveal my secrets in my book *Fearless Author* which also contains handy marketing checklists, lists of links, and other helpful bonuses.

Fearless Author continues to bring me high-paying leads every month on autopilot, and a self-published book in your niche can do the same for you by establishing yourself as an expert and bringing clients to you.

For more information, go to my website http://www.ashleyemmaauthor.com or email me at ashley@ashleyemmaauthor.com.

There is SO much you can do with self-publishing that you can't do with traditional publishing in my opinion, especially if you want to use your book to build your business and bring you leads.

I know many "hybrid" authors who do both self-publishing and traditional publishing. At the time of writing this, my audiobook version of *Undercover Amish* is with my agent, and we hope to find a publisher for it soon.

However, some agents will not consider self-published authors, so keep that in mind.

I highly recommend Self-Publishing School, which is the course that helped get started on my self-publishing journey. This is the course that helped me launch my first book officially and launch my writing career. This course is probably the best investment I made toward my career.

Register for Self-Publishing School's free workshop: How to Go from Blank Page to Bestseller in 90 Days: https://xe172.isrefer.com/go/sps4fta-vts/ashleyemma1

The Best Tools I Recommend for Self-publishing

An Excerpt from my book *Fearless Author*

The first one is KDP Rocket. It can help you create titles for your books by showing you which keywords have the most traffic and the lowest competition, and it has many other useful functions. I always use KDP Rocket to find keywords for my books and use them in my titles and book descriptions to drive more traffic to my books. You can also discover profitable niches and test your book idea to see if it will make money BEFORE you publish it or even write it.

Now KDP Rocket also does category and Amazon keyword research! This is a new feature.

KDP Rocket is currently $97. Totally worth it in my opinion. I use it multiple times a month for my books.

KDP Rocket: https://jvz9.com/c/843169/225041 or www.kdprocket.com

KDROI is a unique software application you install on your internet browser that submits your book promotion to over 32 eBook promotion sites in 15 seconds, and it saves you from spending hours and hours filling out the forms that these sites require. Instead, this software does it all for you with a few clicks. You could hire someone on a site like Fiverr to do this for you, but over time it will save you a lot of money to buy the software once and have it forever. I personally use this software to promote my books on free promotions and 99 cent promotions multiple times a month and it has been a game changer for me. I have multiple books so I save a lot of money. I used to pay someone to do this for me each time, so the software paid for itself in is first few weeks of me using it!

At the time of writing this, KDROI is only $47. You will see how quickly you will make this money back.

KDROI: https://jvz4.com/c/843169/179288 or www.kdroi.com

I use KDSpy to find the best categories on Kindle, and categories are extremely important. It also gets installed right into your browser. Not all authors know this, but currently Amazon lets you have up to 10 categories for eBooks which results in a ton more exposure than only 2 or 3. This software shows you the ranking and revenue for each book in a category with only one click so you can see how competitive it is. It also shows you the best keywords in those categories you are researching, even telling you how competitive the keywords are. This software is a major time saver! I use it for every single book I publish, whether it is my own book or one of my clients', and I don't know what I would do without it.

Currently, this software is also $47. A huge steal!

KDSpy: https://jvz5.com/c/843169/111047 or www.kdspy.com

Amazon ads are a fantastic way to sell more books. The thing is, they are very time consuming and complicated to learn, and it can take a while to see any good results if you do it on your own. Not to mention all the money you can waste trying to test out ads that may only flop.

BookAds is a brand new service that makes profitable Amazon ads for you so you don't have to waste time and money doing it on your own.

Many authors try Amazon ads only to give up quickly, so BookAds will put you way ahead of your competition.

Right now it's only $49 a month plus ad spend which is probably a lot less than what you'd spend if you did it on your own. For example, I spent over four months and hundreds of dollars on experimenting before I found an ad that makes a profit on my book. I only wish BookAds had come out sooner! Now I use BookAds on my book Undercover Amish and plan to hire them to do ads on my other books as well.

BookAds: http://bookads.co/?ref=amishbookwriter@gmail.com

If you do decide to try Amazon ads yourself, check out this free course on Amazon ads from Dave Chesson, creator of KP Rocket: https://kindlepreneur.com/ams-book-advertising-course/

Again, I recommend Self-Publishing School's free workshop: How to Go from Blank Page to Bestseller in 90 Days: https://xe172.isrefer.com/go/sps4fta-vts/ashleyemma1

Vanity Publishing

Vanity publishing is *not* the same as self-publishing or traditional publishing.

Basically, a vanity publisher is a company that you pay to publish your book. Many of them do effectively market your book, but be cautious, because some don't.

None of my author friends who have gone through vanity publishers have sold more than a few dozen books. (You can read these stories in *Fearless Author*.)

If a publisher approaches you online asking if they can publish your book, it is most likely a vanity publisher who just wants your money. Traditional publishers don't work this way. Traditional publisher either require the author to submit their work to them or they will require an agent to submit the author's work, and they only accept a small amount of submissions.

When I was a teenager, I almost signed a publishing contract with a vanity publisher who was recently shut down due to being dishonest. I'm so glad I didn't do it. Do your research.

Writing Contests

A good thing to do before thinking about publishing your book is to submit your writing to contests or try to get short stories published. Two of my manuscripts have been finalists in contests, so when I submitted them to agents and publishers, I was able to mention that. This will give you more credibility as a writer.

You can also get very helpful feedback on your work sometimes, depending on the contest. I've mostly only done contests that are for Maine residents only, but I do recommend Wattpad's writing contests that they have from time to time at http://www.wattpad.com. My book Amish Under Fire was a semi-finalist in their Harlequin's So You Think You Can Write Contest 2015 and received a lot of exposure. If you do an online search for writing contests, you will be able to find plenty. Many of them happen only once a year.

Traditional Publishing

It is VERY hard to get a book traditionally published. Just because you wrote a book, and your mom thinks it is good, doesn't mean it'll be accepted by an agent or traditional publisher. Actually, the chance of getting published is pretty small. I'm not trying to dash your dreams, but only ensure you understand it is very challenging and can take years. Only the very persistent (and talented) make it. One of my editors tried to get published for ten years before he signed a contract. Now he writes for ESPN.

I recently acquired an agent who saw my self-published book on Amazon, saw how successful it was, and asked to represent the audiobook version of my book. This is rare because many agents do not consider self-published authors.

Agents

To get a contract with a major publishing house, you're most likely going to need an agent. There are some that do not require agents, and I'll elaborate on that next. Agents will take a percentage of your profit if you become published, so they only take on authors who look promising to them. If an agent asks you for money up front, stay away.

Check out http://pred-ed.com/ for more info on this.

Here are some resources on where to find a good agent. There are scam artists out there, so be aware that some people will pose as an agent only to try to steal your book. Never send your entire book to anyone that you haven't done your homework on.

The best way to find an agent is to meet them in person at a writer's conference and pitch to them, or have another author write a letter of recommendation for you that they send to their own agent who might be interested in what you write. According to what I learned at a writer's conference, these are two great ways to get your foot in the door.

For the agents you cannot pitch to in person, you will need to send them a query letter. A great way to get an agent's attention is to have an article or short story published, or to have your work win or place in a writing contest. If your writing has won any awards or has been published anywhere, be sure to mention it in your query letter.

Good agent resources:

http://www.writersdigest.com/

http://absolutewrite.com/forums/activity.php?s=d48daa01e0f78dfb53075491f65a8207

http://www.publishersmarketplace.com/

Before you query any agents, make sure you read their guidelines on their website very carefully and spell their name correctly. Agents have personally told me that they hate when authors don't spell their names correctly! I recommend having your submission edited by an editor who specializes in query letters, proposals, and so forth. I recommend Kathy Ide at www.KathyIde.com.

Publishers That Don't Require Agents

If you love writing, sign up for Author's Publish Magazine's email newsletter. (https://www.authorspublish.com/) They give you links to all kinds of writing jobs and publishers looking for material.

They have eBooks that list publishers that don't require agents and some that actually prefer to work only with the author. At the time of this writing, they come out with a new one every year, so the titles change.

I got two publishing contract offers from publishers in the eBook. (I turned them down to self-publish because I make more self-publishing.)

The most recent book is called *The 2017 Guide to Manuscript Publishers,* which you can buy on Amazon if they are no longer giving it away for free by the time you read this: https://www.amazon.com/2017-Guide-Manuscript-Publishers-Traditional-ebook/dp/B073HQJPVS

https://www.authorspublish.com/submit-to-authors-publish-magazine/

Ghostwriting for Clients0

Ghostwriting is in high demand because there are lots of people who want to publish a book, but few have the time, dedication, and know-how to write a book. There are some entrepreneurs who have created six-figure businesses from income generated by sales of ghostwritten eBooks on Amazon.

If you enjoy writing and would like to get paid to help others achieve their dream of having a book published in their name, ghostwriting might be a good fit for you.

You could also ghostwrite blog posts, emails, articles, or short stories for clients. There are many possibilities.

The best way to get started is to publish your own articles, short stories or book. Choose a genre or topic that you can write about easily and is similar to the kind of books that you want to ghostwrite for others. I have a friend who specializes in ghostwriting books on business and history. She is able to drum up lots of repeat clients because she shows clients that she is an expert in these two fields. These topics have become easier for her to write about with each book because she has spent a lot of time studying them.

Once you publish your own book, start marketing yourself as a ghostwriter. Take on a few small, low-paying jobs at first in order to build your portfolio and gain experience. Many clients will not want you to use the material your wrote or them as a sample, so be sure to have some sample work on hand to that you have rights to that you can show potential clients. You can find lots of jobs on websites like Upwork and Fiverr. You can also network in Facebook groups and online forums for Kindle publishers.

Set up your own website that showcases your samples and tells prospective clients more about what you do. Offer discounts for first-time clients. If you don't have the technical know-how to make your website, hire someone to do this for you. Feature testimonials from previous clients on the front page of your website.

Never stop learning. Read every book you can get your hands on about how to write best-selling books. Read books in the niche you want to write in so you can see what is selling well and be exposed to other writing styles. Attend writers' conferences and take classes. If you dedicate yourself to becoming the best writer that you can be, your clients will offer you repeat work and recommend you to their friends.

If you are interested in starting a career ghostwriting books for profit, check out these resources:

Sign up for the free eBook on how to find ghostwriting gigs

http://associationofghostwriters.org/

Article on How to Become a Ghostwriter

https://thewritelife.com/how-to-become-a-ghostwriter/

Not sure what writing niche to specialize in?

https://horkeyhandbook.samcart.com/referral/freelance-writing-niches/RO7AGdsWbyYJMdKj

30 Days or Less to Freelance Writing Success Course:

https://horkeyhandbook.samcart.com/referral/30-Days-or-Less-to-Freelance-Writing-Success/RO7AGdsWbyYJMdKj

Free "How to Become a Freelance Writer" Blogpost:

https://horkeyhandbook.samcart.com/referral/how-to-become-a-paid-freelance-writer/RO7AGdsWbyYJMdKj

Gina Horkey's site:

www.horkeyhandbook.com

https://horkeyhandbook.samcart.com/referral/shop/RO7AGdsWbyYJMdKj

Success Stories:

https://horkeyhandbook.samcart.com/referral/sss/RO7AGdsWbyYJMdKj

Publishing Books For Clients

This section is about how I started Fearless Publishing House (This is BY FAR the most profitable work-at-home job I've ever done):

How to Start Your Publishing Business: A Quick-Start Guide

People will gladly pay to have their book published by a professional. Clients come to me, and if you follow my advice, they will be asking you to publish their books too.

Let me first say that my company Fearless Publishing House is not a vanity publisher. We are very selective about who we take on as clients. We get their input and walk them through the whole self-publishing process, and they keep 100% of their rights and royalties.

I also coach clients on how to self-publish their book so they can do it themselves for multiple books while having complete control over the entire process. Once you feel experienced enough after publishing several books, you can also offer coaching to your clients.

If you want to start publishing books for clients, I recommend that you follow these guidelines:

- Genuinely care about each and every one of your clients and do everything you can to help them and their books succeed. Not only will you get great testimonials, but your client's satisfaction should be priority.

- Be very selective about the books you publish. Only publish the books you think will be successful. This protects both you and your clients. If you publish a book that you know isn't the best it can be, your client will just end up unhappy with the results when it doesn't sell well. Also, you don't want to put your publishing company name on low-quality books. If someone submits a book to you and it just needs more work, ask the author to spend more time on it and then resubmit it to you in the future.

- Have your clients buy their own ISBNs so they can sell their books wherever they want (www.bowker.com).

- Retain no rights to the cover, manuscript, or anything you provide them. It is your client's to do whatever they want with. They should also keep all of their royalties.

If you are self-publishing several of your own books and investing in training, you will most likely have the experience needed to publish for clients. If you are honest and hard-working, this can be a great way to make a living.

You can turn your $0.99 or $2.99 eBook into a tool that brings you thousands of dollars in client work.

So many people in this world *want* to write and publish a book and have always dreamed of becoming an author. They don't know how to get started or what process to take, and the whole publishing process confuses and overwhelms them.

They might just need some guidance and you could coach them through the publishing process. You could also do this for your clients and charge around $2,000 to $4,000 to teach them everything they need to know to write and publish a bestselling book.

What's more, there are so many people who need a book to use as the "ultimate business card" in their business.

They can use a book to hand out to potential clients, proving they are experts and getting way ahead of their competitors.

Depending on what niche they are in, they can make their money back with one or a few clients (for example: realtors, lawyers, surgeons, or life coaches).

You can help them write it, or charge even more when you write it for them, for around $15,000 to $20,000. Yes, this is a realistic rate.

This is what I do full time, and I'm making great money doing it. In fact, I hardly work in my salon anymore, and I've cut back on other things in my life so I can focus on this.

At the time of writing this, I typically make between $2,500-$10,000 per client, depending on how many books they want to publish or how much writing I do for them.

Sometimes you might only make $400 for a quick marketing package that takes an hour or two to schedule the promotions.

Here is a quick overview of how you can get started publishing books for clients:

1. **Learn all you can about publishing** both Kindle books and paperback books on Amazon. I recommend publishing at least one or two bestselling books of your own. In order to do this, you could read books on self-publishing like *Fearless Author* (http://a.co/5IqzNDR), which explains in step-by-step detail how I published and launched all of my bestselling books, or *High Performance Paperback* (http://a.co/hZPKoR1) by Jim Molinelli and Ray Brehm. If you have at least one or two bestselling books of your own, your clients will see you as a publishing expert, and at that point you should know enough to provide them with publishing services. (Your books do not have to be bestsellers, but it does give you more credibility.)

2. **Get more clients on autopilot through your eBooks (this strategy has made me thousands of dollars).** In my book about self-publishing, *Fearless Author,* I put my

ScheduleOnce link in the front and back of my book. Along with this link, I offer readers a free consultation with me that they can book using ScheduleOnce—no secretary required—using https://www.scheduleonce.com/pricing?refcode=AEP818.

They are then redirected to a form where I ask them about their book, goals, and budget. They are required to fill out this book submission form and submit the first chapter or so of their book, a book description, what their goals are for their book, or their book idea.

This is how I've gotten most my clients so far. It is very easy to set up. You can look at their submission, and if it's not a good fit, you can cancel the appointment.

Once you get busy, you can pick and choose the people you want to work with before even speaking to them. By requiring them to submit their book information to you, and letting them know you only pick the most-qualified prospects, they take speaking with you much more seriously and respect you as an expert even more.

Plus, it filters out all the serious prospects from the uncommitted prospects. Almost everyone who books a free consultation with me has already read my book or watched my webinar about self-publishing, and they know they want to go forward with the self-publishing process. They are thoroughly vetted before you talk to them.

3. **Make a list of all the services** you can provide and put it in your book and on your website. Here are some examples:

- Coaching
- Setting up Mailchimp
- Building your email list
- Create your website
- Designing and installing your pop-up form
- Outlining and writing help
- Helping you write your book
- Transcription
- Proofreading and editing
- Formatting
- Cover design help

- Publishing to KDP on Amazon
- Writing a gripping book description
- Finding the perfect keywords and categories for maximum exposure
- Launching the eBook
- Marketing packages
- Getting reviews
- Getting editorial reviews
- Teaching you how to keep sales up
- Helping you get local book signings
- Helping you get on your local news
- Amazon ads help
- Creating paperback books to sell on Amazon, put in local bookstores and libraries, and give to clients and friends

There is more you could offer as you gain more experience.

4. **Make a few publishing packages** using your list of services. Here are some examples:

- Basic Publishing Package (a basic eBook publishing package that includes all of the production aspects, such as formatting and covers, with some marketing): $2,000.
- Bestseller Package (an eBook publishing package that is mostly extensive marketing and a launch): $2,500.
- Standard eBook Package (this package has extensive marketing and a launch plan. It also covers all of the eBook production such as formatting and cover options. You'd also help them build their website and email list): $4,500.
- Professional Publishing Package (the Standard Package but also for a print book as well as an eBook): $6,000
- The Ultimate Publishing Package (everything in the Standard Package PLUS you'd ghostwrite the book for the client): $10,000+.
- Plus make a few marketing packages that **clients can choose from and reorder on a regular basis** to keep book sales up or offer custom packages.

5. **Find people you can outsource most of your work to** on websites like https://www.fiverr.com/. You can outsource most of this work and still make a huge profit. It may take you some trial and error to find sellers who provide quality work that you like, so test gigs out on your own books and create lists of your favorite sellers who create book covers, market books, write descriptions, etc. Always double check or edit the work if necessary, especially for written work like book descriptions.

6. **Start small.** I recommend charging $500 to $1,000 for your first basic publishing package then raise your prices as you take on more work. You can even do it for free if you want and have the client pay for the expenses.

7. **If you live in a small town, find clients by contacting people locally who own their own business** like chiropractors, lawyers, dentists, realtors, health professionals, etc. You can find these through an online search in your area. Here's a tip: Contact the businesses that advertise on the back of the phonebook or place large ads in the newspapers.

   Or you can contact businesses that do other sorts of advertising such as Google ads. These businesses want more clients and probably have money to invest. Call or email them and politely approach them. Introduce yourself and let them know that if they had a book, they would be light years ahead of their competition. Tell them that instead of handing their potential clients a standard business card, they could hand their clients a book with their name on it that shows that they are a true expert in their niche. Depending on what they charge, they could make their money back with just one or two clients, and the book will continue to **bring them business for years to come.** How incredible is that?

8. If you have no testimonials, **show them** your own book as an example and explain how they can use a book to get more clients.

9. **No matter where you live, branch out by finding more clients online.** Find websites for bloggers, coaches, copywriters, marketers, consultants, fitness professionals, etc., and send them a professional email asking them if they have ever considered writing a book to establish themselves as an authority in their niche and bring them more clients. Keep it short and don't include pricing. That should only be discussed if they are interested. If they reply to your email, then offer them to book a free call with you with your ScheduleOnce link at https://www.scheduleonce.com/pricing?refcode=AEP818.

   Here's an example of an email you could send to potential clients who are not already authors. Notice the subject line. That is important!

   Example email:

   Subject: Trying to get in touch with (their name)

   Dear (their name),

Your website is beautiful! Have you ever considered writing a book to establish yourself as even more of an authority in your niche and bring you more clients on autopilot using a scheduling software?

If you're interested, just hit reply and we can chat.

Thanks,

(your name)

10. **You can also find authors on Amazon** who need book services like a new cover, new description, marketing, editing, or completely republishing their book. Just click on different categories of book on Amazon (I suggest starting with eBooks) and click the last few pages of each category. These are the books that are selling the least amount in that category. Look for their email on their Amazon Author Central profile and send them an email like this. If they reply to your email, then offer them to book a free call with you using your ScheduleOnce link. Again, notice the subject line in this sample email:

Subject: (Put the title of their book here. This will grab their attention.)

Dear (author name),

I found your book (add title here) on Amazon and noticed it has the potential to be ranking much higher. I'm a publisher for self-published authors and I also do marketing, book covers, editing, etc. I think with a new cover and a rewritten description along with some marketing, your book could be ranking much higher on the charts.

Just hit reply if you have any questions. I'd love to chat.

Sincerely,

(your name)

11. If a person has enough content on their website, offer to compile it for them into a book, requiring little to no work on their part. You could also offer to write it for them or help them write it for a larger fee. Show them how your own book gets you clients. Point out testimonials from your past clients. When they see how a book can bring them more business and ultimately make them more money, you should have no problem getting clients. You can also search for potential clients in Facebook groups for specific niches. Linked In is also a great resource to connect with potential clients. Get to know a prospective client if possible before mentioning your services. Make sure you always add value first when posting or contacting them. Don't spam anyone.

12. **Whatever you do, put the client first and give them as much value as you can.** Always be honest and straight forward. Do not promise your client that they will make a million

dollars in book royalties. Over-deliver on your part, do your best, and they will recommend you to their friends. You can also offer a referral program.

13. **After you finish publishing projects for clients, collect testimonials for your website and email signature.** Create a logo, create a professional website, and create quality business cards. Treat this like a real business and be confident, and you will attract what you put out. This might be obvious, but I think it's important.

The information I have provided here should be enough to at least get you going if you are interested in publishing books for clients.

However, if you would like help or just have some questions about starting your own self-publishing company, set up a free strategy session with me by emailing me at ashley@ashleyemmaauthor.com. I'd be happy to help and give you some guidance.

Starting Your Own Salon And Doing Wedding Services

My At-Home Salon Business

(I know this isn't for everyone. If you are not interested in doing hair, feel free to skip this section. I cover how to do other types of wedding services in the next section.)

Cosmetology school is expensive, and you must be a licensed cosmetologist to work in a salon.

However, since this is a book about working at home, I will share about how I started my in-home salon.

I grew up with a salon in my parents' house. My mom did hair, and my grandmother also had her own salon, so I'm a third-generation cosmetologist. I went to hair school when I was 18, right after high school, and graduated early at the top of my class.

When my husband and I built our house a few years ago, we knew we wanted a salon in it, so we built it into the house. Adding a salon into your house after it is built can be very difficult because there is a list of laws and requirements that your home salon needs to meet, like having its own bathroom and separate entrance. I recommend planning ahead and doing it the most cost-efficient way: building the salon when you build your house.

When we built my salon, I already had a full clientele to bring in from when I worked at my mom's salon, so I had an advantage. If you are going to booth rent or build your own salon, the best way to do it is if you already have a full clientele so you know you will make your money back. It also depends on the area you live in and how much traffic you can get. Also, the zoning laws where we live allowed us to build a salon here. You'd need to look into the zoning laws in your area.

I love having a salon in my home because I can work with the kids nearby. I used to work without a babysitter when I had only one child. She was a very mellow baby and would sit in her swing or play in her playpen while I worked, but now that we have a baby boy and my daughter is a toddler, I only work when a babysitter or my husband is watching them. In fact, I've cut my hours back to only one night a week to devote more time to publishing my books and my clients' books.

Now that I self-publish books full time and make ten times more money doing that, I have sent most of my clientele to my mom's salon or my friend's salon down the street. It took me several years to build this business, and I like doing hair, but I love creating books so much more, and it pays much better. It has been bittersweet to gradually stop doing hair.

Sometimes you have to quit doing things you like in order to make time for doing the things you love, but it's worth it.

Doing Wedding Services

(If you're not interested in doing wedding services, feel free to skip this section.)

There are many other types of wedding services you can do besides doing hair.

Keep in mind that you do need a cosmetology license to legally do hair for weddings, but you do not need a license to do some of the other things like photography, for example. But you'll need a high-quality camera and great photography skills, of course, and training helps.

I've been doing hair and makeup for weddings in the summertime, which is the most profitable part of my hair salon business. I usually do the weddings with my mom (also a licensed cosmetologist with her own salon) or my sister-in-law who is in training to become a hairstylist, so it is really fun. We charge extra to travel to the wedding party. Doing wedding hairstyles is my favorite part of doing hair.

For fun, feel free to check out my salon Facebook page with photos of my hair creations: https://www.facebook.com/ashleyssalonbiddeford/

I also have an Instagram account on which I sometimes post pictures of my hairstyles, and if you can keep up with it, Instagram is a great way to spread the word about your services. But I mostly stick to posting my pictures on Facebook and Wedding Wire just because I'm so busy and I'm not looking for new clients anymore.

I usually make $500-$1,000 a day doing hair and makeup for wedding parties and traveling to them, depending on if I work alone or not and if I have more than one wedding booked that day. We advertise on www.weddingwire.com, which has brought us tons of leads this year—we have booked 26 weddings for this summer through Wedding Wire. It is a bit pricey, but my mother and I split the cost and we made a profit with the first two weddings we did, so it is well worth it!

Update: I stopped paying for advertising our second year on Wedding Wire because I don't need any more clients. I still have a free profile on their site, but I am no longer on the first page and do not have a profile photo. I don't get as much exposure as the vendors who are paying, but I still get leads weekly because I have built up a solid profile with several reviews and a good reputation.

So, you may only need to pay for the first year, but it depends on many factors like where you live and how many clients you already have who will advertise for you through word of mouth.

Interested brides contact us through the Wedding Wire Clients messaging app after seeing our Wedding Wire profile, so it is simple to keep track of all of our conversations with brides in this one place. My younger twin sisters are advertising their cupcake business Twin.Cakes (yes, that is how they spell it) on Wedding Wire.

The great thing about this business is it is very part time and seasonal. Most of my wedding work takes place on Fridays and Saturdays from June-September, so it fits into my busy schedule. Depending on where you live, you might do most of your work in the summer. I hardly do any weddings in the winter here in Maine.

Wedding Wire is a website that can be used to advertise any wedding-related business such as cakes, catering, venues, and photography. They have a great support team who will provide you with free online training about how to get more clients and they will answer your questions.

A few tips for maximizing your Wedding Wire profile:

- Ask all your clients for a review after you have completed the service. For weddings, wait at least two weeks so the bride is home from her honeymoon. Wedding Wire currently allows you to give a thank you gift for reviews, but you can't buy reviews. (Make sure this hasn't changed before you try this.) I sent the brides who left me reviews a $5 gift card to Wal-Mart. Each time you get a review, your visibility increases so you'll get more people on your page.

- When potential clients ask about your services, there is no need to type a new list of prices and your general information each time. I talked to over 80 brides within a few months, so that can be time consuming. Instead, type your general information, FAQs, prices, and links to your contract, photos, and reviews. Keep it on your phone in a place where you can easily access it. I keep mine in my Evernote app and copy and paste it into the email or message that the potential client sends me. I personalize it to each person. For example, include their name or mention the wedding location.

- Use Google Forms to make a contract for your clients to sign when they book with you.

- Do not book anyone until they pay a deposit. I use PayPal and credit cards over the phone to accept deposits.

- Add as many photos as you can to your profile and use the best ones as your featured photos. Choose one of your best photos for your profile photo as well.

- Wedding Wire also has a feature where you can easily make videos using your photos. Not everyone does this, so make sure you take the time to do it. The more complete your profile is, the more exposure you'll get.

- There is a section where you can create a "deal" and offer a discount on your services if your clients use a coupon code. When you do this, it makes a little icon in the corner of your profile picture that says "deal" that will make you stand out among your competitors. Many vendors don't know how to do this or know about it at all, so if you do, you will attract more potential clients.

- Keep your prices updated and put a link to your website or Facebook page as well.

Here is our Wedding Wire profile if you'd like to see what it looks like (this link may change if we do not continue advertising with them): https://www.weddingwire.com/biz/ashleys-salon-biddeford/cdb5095e4f9071ab.html

Below is an example of the document I send to the brides and potential clients who reach out to me inquiring about my wedding services. This is mostly done over email.

It took me several months and a lot of trial and error to figure out the best way to respond to leads, so I hope you can use what I have learned to take a shortcut.

A few tips when responding to brides and potential clients:

- Include a link to your reviews and photos.

- Provide pricing.

- Be very specific.

- Always end with an open-ended question.

- You can copy and paste your response each time, but make sure to personalize it to each bride or potential client. Include their name and mention their wedding date or venue.

- Pricing will depend on the area you live in. Look up prices at salons near you and try to be in the same range as them. Once you get busy enough, make sure you raise your prices.

Feel free to use this document and tweak it to make it your own. This document could be used for most wedding services and can also be used for other sites similar to Wedding Wire.

My sisters just used this for their cupcake business and changed the hair pricing to their cupcake pricing, swapped my email and name for theirs, etc.

You will notice a few links at the end. One is to our terms in Google Docs, one is to our reviews and photos on Wedding Wire, and one is to our contract on Google Forms. (If I ever completely stop doing hair in the future, these links may change. I will also include our terms below.)

Here is the document I send to potential clients on Wedding Wire:

Thank you for contacting Ashley's Salon! Congrats on your engagement. :) We are available that day and would be happy to travel to you.

If you choose us, you'll be making a great choice! We won the Couples' Choice Awards 2017 for the top 5% of all Wedding Wire vendors!

Our updo's are gorgeous and will stay in for 2 days, and our makeup will last all day and all night.

Booking with us is quick and easy! We accept PayPal and credit card (over the phone) for deposits. We also accept cash and checks on the wedding day for the remaining balance.

Our contract is electronic and takes only a few minutes to fill out and submit so your wedding date can be secured quickly.

Here is some basic information about our prices and services.

Trial prices are not included with wedding services. These are separate.

Our prices are:

-Bride's hairstyle or trial: $90

-All other hairstyles (updo's, half up styles, blowouts, etc.) or trials: $75

-Bride's makeup or trial: $65 including false eyelashes (they look very natural)

-All other makeup applications or trial: $55 including false eyelashes

-Travel fee: $2 a mile each way (from 534 South Street, Biddeford, Maine to where you will be getting ready no the wedding day.)

-Assistant fee (only when an assistant is needed) $100

-Deposit: 50% of the estimated total, including travel fee. The deposit is due when you choose to officially book the wedding with us and is nonrefundable. We accept credit card payments over the phone (***) ***-**** or PayPal to ashleys.salon.maine@gmail.com only for deposits so we can book you right away.

Because we receive so many inquiries each week, we will not be able to officially book your wedding date until the deposit is paid. Also, because we often book two weddings in one day, we will need to know how many people in your party will be getting our services as soon as possible so we can plan around it.

A few other important things:

-The prices for hairstyles are a flat fee, no matter what the hairstyle is.

-Our updo's last 2 days and makeup will last all day and all night! We use a special Lock and Seal product mixed with our makeup and finish with a setting spray.

-We highly recommend a trial run so that you will know exactly which hairstyle and makeup look you want and so you know how it will look on you in advance.

Thanks so much and please call or text (***) ***-**** for any questions!

Have you read our reviews? Here's a link to them: https://m.weddingwire.com/reviews/ashleys-salon-biddeford/cdb5095e4f9071ab

Would you like to book a trial or would you like to see photos of our work?

https://docs.google.com/document/d/1xGO7yAT9QYUYqeaq__l9ZTAqs4TqtL8I-SoixFoCJPU

More photos:

https://m.facebook.com/pg/ashleyssalonbiddeford/photos/?ref=page_internal&mt_nav=1

Here is the link to our Google docs version of our terms and wedding day info.

https://docs.google.com/document/d/1sGiXgrbh0IJMwZOk9g55zNDxu4NuVbyOTCud5-ptNf0/edit?usp=sharin

Here is the link to our contract if you want to look at it: https://goo.gl/forms/886jHUDk0F1Hi6kP2

I'll need to know what time you need to be ready by (this is a time separate from when the wedding starts) so I can determine if I'll need an assistant.

Do you have any questions?

-Ashley

Below is a copy of our terms.

Notice how I also have the contract, pricing, and other important information included in the terms as well as in the response I send to brides. This makes this information very accessible.

Again, this can be used for most wedding services. Your conditions will depend on what services you do. For example, instead of saying that everyone's hair must be clean and dry, my sisters changed that part to say that they are not responsible for what happens to the cupcakes after they are delivered.

Again, feel free to use this and customize it to your own business:

Ashley's Salon's Terms and Wedding Day Info

(***) ***-****

Bridal Party Information

Thank you for considering Ashley's Salon to help you look and feel your best on one of the most joyous days of your life. Your confidence in how you look on this day is very important to us!

Please feel free to call or text Ashley directly with any questions at (***) ***-**** or email ashleys.salon.maine@gmail.com.

Contract Information:

Please see the Google Forms electronic Contract that you can fill out and return to us online. If you do not have one yet, please click this link and fill it out so we can officially book and secure your wedding date for you.

https://docs.google.com/forms/d/1dcbZwaKES-BMKjMbnV5wpvPySgaXg0rcUjHwAXfXndQ/edit?usp=forms_home&ths=true

Prices:

- *Updo/any hairstyle: $75*
- *Makeup: $55 (includes false eyelashes)*
- *Bride's updo/hairstyle: $90*
- *Bride's makeup: $65 (includes false eyelashes)*
- *Updos or hairstyles for flowergirls/children: $45-$55*
- *Travel fee: $2 a mile round trip/each way (from our salon address to where you will be getting ready on the wedding day.)*

(Please note that many half up styles and wearing hair down in curls require as much time and work or more as an updo and may be the same price as an updo.)

Stylists may charge extra for blow drying wet hair unless that client is scheduled to have a Blowout.

Deposit: 50% of the estimated total, including travel fee. The deposit is due when you choose to officially book the wedding with us and is nonrefundable. We accept credit card payments over the phone (***) ***-****, PayPal to ashleys.salon.maine@gmail.com only for deposits so that we can book you right away.

Because we receive so many inquires each week, we will not be able to officially book your wedding date until the deposit is paid. Also, because we often book two weddings on the same day, we will need to know an approximate number of how many people in your party will be needing services as soon as possible so we can plan around it.

Trial Runs

Trial runs are optional but HIGHLY recommended so you know exactly what makeup and hairstyle you want on your wedding day and what it will look like. Almost every bride we have serviced has booked a trial run. It also helps the stylist know exactly how to do it on the wedding day, which will save both of you time and stress. A trial run should be booked within one month of the wedding so that the stylist has it still fresh in their mind for the wedding day, but this is not required. Please bring any hair accessories for the wedding to the trial such as veils or tiaras.

Call or text Ashley at (***) ***-****or email ashleys.salon.maine@gmail.com to book your trial run!

Our Terms

We will not be able to secure your wedding date for you until we receive your deposit. For deposits we accept PayPal and credit card over the phone so that we can receive your deposit quicker and then book you right away. We cannot reserve your wedding date while waiting for a check or cash in the mail. (On the wedding day we accept these forms of payment as well as cash or check.)

The signed contract is due when the deposit is paid.

We often get two different inquiries from different brides for the same wedding date, and it doesn't matter who emails us first, we have to book whoever pays the deposit first.

We also may book two weddings in one day if the timing of both weddings coordinate.

We book up very quickly and schedule clients on a first come first serve basis, so we will need to keep your wedding date open until we receive your deposit. Thanks for understanding!

We also work with assistants from other salons who also book up quickly, so if we do not receive the contract and deposit after a few weeks of penciling you in, we may not be able to still secure the date for you, but we will of course try our best!

Please fill out and mail the contract to the address at the top of the form or fill out digitally and email to ashleys.salon.maine@gmail.com.

Payment in full is due on the day of the wedding or a late fee may be charged. If one of the clients in the bridal party does not pay for their service(s) in full and for some reason we cannot collect payment for that service, the bride will be charged for that service.

If one of the stylists has an injury or personal emergency or for some reason cannot perform services, we will either replace them with another stylist or may need to come earlier or ask for more time for getting the bridal party ready.

If for some reason no stylists can perform services on the wedding day, all fees will be refunded and we will do our best to find you another option.

If there are ferry fees, parking fees, etc., the bride is responsible for reimbursing Ashley's Salon on the day of the wedding.

Ashley's Salon and its stylists will not be held liable for any injuries on the wedding day.

If any of the clients in the bridal party decide to not have the services done on the wedding day that are listed in the contract order form, they will still be charged for 50% of the service price. (This is to prevent multiple people from backing out after we arrive, which would result in a substantial loss of profit on our end.) We arrive planning on doing a certain amount of people, and when some clients back out last minute or do not arrive on time, we still have to pay our assistants the amount originally promised to them. This rule may also apply if someone shows up late or no one is ready to begin at the designated time we are supposed to start and there is not enough time left to finish everyone.

We do take credit cards, but prefer cash on the wedding day. We also accept checks. We will charge a 3% fee for wedding day credit card payments to cover processing fees we will be charged with which add up quickly for multiple services.

Cancellations and no shows: Wedding parties who make cancellations fewer than 14 days of the wedding date or are no shows will still be charged 50% of the estimated bridal party's total so we can still pay our assistants.

Late arrivals: Bridal parties who arrive more than one hour late on the wedding day without contacting Ashley's Salon by calling or texting (***) ***-**** will be considered a no show and the credit card we have on file will be charged 50% of the estimated total. Or, if we stay and do the wedding, we may just not have enough time to finish everyone's hair and makeup.

If the party arrives late or some of the clients arrive late, we cannot guarantee that we will have time to do everyone's hair and makeup as originally planned.

If a client has wet or damp hair and is scheduled for an updo but not a Blowout, the stylists may charge extra for blow drying time.

Important Wedding Day Information

The stylists will plan on arriving early to allow time to set up.

The stylists will need a designated no walk-through traffic area to work that has tables, chairs and outlets. Please have an area picked out and cleared in advance.

Please have at least three clients ready to have their hair or makeup done right away when our stylists arrive on the morning of the wedding so that we do not have to wait as they decide who wants to go first. This is very important so that we do not run behind, since we have a limited amount of time.

The bridesmaids and attendants should decide on a tentative order of who will get their hair and makeup done before the wedding day so that the stylists do not spend time waiting between clients. We usually work on two or three people at a time and the rotation needs to keep going without wait time in between in order to have plenty of time for everyone.

If no one is ready to start when we arrive and we have to wait while the wedding party decides who wants to go first, this can put us very behind schedule and some clients may not end up getting their hair or makeup done. The client(s) who we are unable to finish, in this type of situation, would still be charged for 50% of their service fee that was on the contract order form so we can still pay our assistants.

Our updos stay in 2-3 days and our makeup lasts all day and all night because we use a setting spray, so it does not make a difference as to how long it will last if the client has their hair and makeup done early in the morning or later in the day.

If anyone not on the contract order form decides that they do want hair or makeup done last minute, we will absolutely be happy to try to accommodate them, if time permits!

Please ask everyone to have clean and dry hair.

We ask that everyone who is getting their hair done on the wedding day has clean and 100% dry hair.

Dirty hair, contrary to popular belief, does not hold a curl well, will not stay in an updo, and looks greasy and flat.

It takes more time to curl and recurl the hair because it falls limp very quickly, and we will have to use a lot of extra product and dry shampoos to try to make it look clean. Because of all this extra time and product, we will charge an extra $10 for each person with dirty hair.

We recommend washing your hair the day before so it is completely dry.

We want your hair to stay in as long as possible and to look absolutely fabulous, so we have these rules in place to protect both of us.

Please ask everyone who is getting updos, half up styles or curls to not wash their hair on the wedding day unless they have scheduled a Blowout. Clients with wet hair will slow down the stylists, and the stylists may charge extra for any blow drying. (The hair has to be 100% dry in order for it to curl.) The stylist may not have time to do an updo or style if they have to blow dry the hair. Also, hair washed the same day will not hold an updo as well as hair that was washed the day or night before.

Please ask everyone to wear button-up or zip-up shirts so they do not damage their hair or makeup when changing clothes.

Please let bridesmaids and attendants know that if they have pictures of what hairstyles or makeup looks that they want (if everyone is getting different styles) we can copy the pictures. We will all be on the same page this way, but it is optional.

***

Thank you again for choosing Ashley's Salon! Your satisfaction is very important to us. If you have any questions or concerns at all, please do not hesitate to call or text Ashley at (***) ***-****. Or email ashleys.salon.maine@gmail.com.

We are excited to help you and your bridal party look and feel their best on your special day!

How to Sell Homemade Cakes

By Ashley Emma and Pawan N.

I interviewed my friend Pawan about the businesses he has successfully started. He has sold homemade cakes, made homemade cards, and has done online tutoring.

In this section, I will share his strategies and tips with you.

Here are a few tips Pawan found useful to share for selling cakes.

1. Start out small and gain as much experience as possible. With cakes, unlike with some other products, you will need plenty of experience in selling and baking a consistent and a delicious product every time.

    Start today. Let your neighbors and social circle know that you are selling cakes. Even if you start out baking for friends and family for free or a discount, deliver perfectly from your first order.

2. Create beautiful, unique, innovative designs and most importantly, leave people in amazement. Make it your goal to create something unique and special that will cause every client to remember you and you will get referrals.

3. Sell your cakes at craft fairs or local festivals where you can hand out samples and business cards. These will encourage people to buy your cakes or possibly contact you for future orders.

4. Make sure you carry your phone with you at all times. Remember, a missed call could be lost business because sometimes people order from whichever business they reach first. Be there when opportunity comes looking for you.

    Also, carry business cards and give them to as many people as you can.

5. Help people find you. Most of Pawan's customers are people who were referred to him by previous buyers, friends, or friends of his friends. Unless you know a lot about advertising, your best bet is to rely on people who have tried your cakes and let them spread the word. You could offer them incentives like 50% off a cake every time they refer someone to you, or something like that.

6. Use social media. From big businesses to small ones, presence on social media is important in today's market, and it's free marketing. Make a Facebook business page, start posting photos of your cakes, post prices with other information, and see what happens.

7. Run a Facebook contest by posting some pictures of your cake creations with your business name, and say what the prize will be and on what date you will pick a name. Make sure you use your business Facebook page to do this.

   For example, to enter your contest, people must share your post, tag someone who likes cake, and "like" your business page. Pick a date and say that you will randomly select one person who entered, and make a big announcement of who the winner is on that day. As a prize you could give away some cake catering (like a cake and cupcakes) or cake baking lessons. These are just some ideas to get you thinking.

   Running a contest like this will give you more exposure to people who specifically like cake. It will grow your following and the number of people who "like" your Facebook page who you can then market to later on through posts on your Facebook page.

8. Hire a delivery person. You might be baking quality cakes, but without a delivery person, you won't be able to grow your business. Discuss their rates and vehicle expenses up front. Be sure that the person you hire is punctual and reliable enough to get your cakes to the customer without any damage.

9. Manage your time and orders. After making an impact on his local target market, the most challenging part Pawan faced was managing his time and orders. If you have baked cakes, you know it's not a five-minute task. It requires patience and preparation. However, orders don't come in a planned manner. Your customers could ask for a cake immediately or request that it be home-delivered at midnight.

10. Remember to take time off or else you might compromise your health, which could impact your work. An unhappy customer due to a poor product because you are tired or sick is bad for business.

11. Check with your local government to make sure that you have all necessary licenses and permits: https://www.sba.gov/blogs/so-youd-start-home-based-baking-business-now-what

In conclusion, if you are passionate about making cakes then sales will probably follow. You just need to advertise your work by using the above strategies and have faith in your abilities.

If a cake business sounds like something you would like learn more about, check out the following resources:

Small Business Administration Article:

https://www.sba.gov/blogs/so-youd-start-home-based-baking-business-now-what

Cake Business Owners Club Article:

https://bakingbusinessschool.com.ng/category/how-to-have-a-profitable-cake-business/

How to Sell Homemade Greeting Cards

By Ashley Emma and Pawan N.

When it comes to greeting cards, personalizing the content is very important. Often buyers are left with choosing a card with good design but not the message they would have wanted or vice versa.

If you are an artsy person, selling homemade greeting cards might be the right fit for you.

Here are my friend Pawan's tips on how one should start selling handmade greeting cards.

1. Know your purpose. Warren Buffet once said, "Risk comes from not knowing what you're doing." If you really want to sell your cards, you will have to be crystal clear about your decision and really commit. Don't bother with any half-hearted attempts. Any successful business, regardless of what you are providing, requires dedication, commitment, and persistence.

2. Figure out how much you can commit. How much time, energy, and money can you invest in your business? Can you sacrifice your weekends?

   Pawan says, "From Friday night till Monday morning I made cards with different designs and themes. Every day after returning from the office I worked on them."

   So, as you can see, this takes your time, energy, and resources. Buying lots of crayons, pens, card material, charts, tiny decorative materials, and glue is important as well as having an organized space to keep it all.

3. Determine who your target market is. Who are your buyers? What are they looking for? What price are they willing to pay? What are they currently buying, and how can you serve them better? Do they buy online or in local stores? The answers to all of these questions will show who you should be marketing your cards to.

4. Decide if you want to sell them locally, online, or both. For example, you could open an Etsy store or try to get your cards into online gift shops.

5. Use social media. In this era of social media and online marketing, reaching your audience is not a difficult task. Whether you plan to serve people living in your area, or reach a huge audience on the Internet, you need to have a social media presence.

   The first thing you can do is create your social media page on websites like Facebook, Instagram and so on. Ask your friends to share and spread the word widely. Keep adding good articles and posts to your pages. Always add photos of your sold cards and cards you would like to use to attract customers. Many people may contact you due to posts you share with pictures of your work. If you own a website, make sure to add good SEO articles.

6. Sell your cards at craft fairs and other events. When people see a brand selling at fairs or events, they trust the credibility of the seller. Don't forget to hand out a lot of flyers and business cards with your contact information and social media links.

7. Make your customers happy. The best form of marketing is word-of-mouth marketing. Make sure to please your buyer by selling a quality product.

8. Never deliver late.

9. If you have a bulk order, always make sure to give a bulk discount. In the end a happy and satisfied customer will spread the word about your card and encourage their social circles to buy from you.

Selling isn't an easy job. You may face lots of challenges but not losing hope and being positive about your work is the key.

If you are interested in turning your homemade greeting cards into a home business, this article will give you a ton of resources on how to get started:

http://kateharperblog.blogspot.com/2013/09/venues-for-selling-greeting-cards-online.html

Tips and Tricks for Succeeding in Online Tutoring

Online tutoring is a rapidly growing industry. I asked Pawan about what he learned along the way on his teaching journey, and this is what he shared with me.

The hardships and challenges in an online tutoring program are just as significant as the ones in standard classroom teaching. Here are some tips for succeeding in online tutoring:

1. Always be on time. Pawan told me being punctual is just as important for an online teacher or tutor as it is for a classroom teacher. Being late is unprofessional and never acceptable.

2. Remember that you are not just competing with tutors in your area. You're competing with tutors around the world. Therefore, you need to be the best you can be. Never stop learning about the subjects that you are teaching.

3. Never promise what you can't deliver. Tell your clients exactly what to expect when they work with you. Offer honest testimonials from previous students.

4. Have your curriculum, syllabus, and training materials ready before you look for clients. In most cases, people will ask you for this information up front. If you are not able to answer questions about your materials, you will have trouble finding clients.

5. Find an online platform that connects you with potential clients. Many tutors find it challenging to get their first clients. However, there are many sites and apps that allow you to find students based on your competency and skillset. Share your email address and website details on social media platforms and forums. One of Pawan's students approached him after she read his comment on www.Quora.com.

    If you don't want to rely on your website alone to bring customers, then you will need to go and find them.

    If you decide to go with online websites that help you find clients, then you have to be willing to pay a hefty amount of money as a commission to the website and play by their rules.

6. Find a reliable payment method. You can use www.PayPal.com, www.Stripe.com, www.Moneygram.com, or www.Payoneer.com. Just remember, you can be dealing with people from any part of the world, so you'll want to offer payment methods that work for students everywhere.

7. Mark your calendars. This is probably the best and most efficient way to keep track of your routine. Making a schedule on your calendar is important because it helps you remain

punctual and not double book yourself.

8. Advertise your services. You may have seen posts about a discounted class starting soon. This is a very good strategy to follow when you want to attract more clients.

Online learning is growing in popularity, and so is the potential. "I have been providing online tutoring sessions for the past three years and I can say with certainty that online tutoring is going to stay as one of the most used services in the near future," Pawan says.

Teach Classes Online

Like online tutoring, teaching classes online is also another great way to make money.

I interviewed my friend Samantha who teaches classes online so I could share her advice with you.

Instead of sticking to only academic classes, you can teach classes on almost any subject from arts and crafts to self-confidence or making money online.

You can teach independently or for a university.

Online teaching positions with a university are not easy to come by and typically require a master's or doctorate degree. You can search for and apply to these jobs on any major job website like www.Monster.com or by going directly to the university website.

However, if you don't have an advanced degree and you want to teach online, there are still options available to you. There are several tutoring websites that are looking for teachers to help students learn everything from Algebra to Zoology.

Teaching English to students all over the world is in very high demand. Some companies require that you have a teaching license, and some do not, so pay close attention to the requirements when applying.

Check out https://www.teachaway.com/online-teaching-jobs.

In many other cases you will not need a degree, but make sure before applying for any positions.

You can check out this comprehensive website for more information on how to land a remote teaching gig:

https://www.teachaway.com/online-teaching-jobs

Another option is to create your own online classes on a subject that you are passionate about. Some people are making six-figure incomes from creating online classes alone.

"Offering an online class can also be an extra stream of income for any professional. In addition to the income, it automatically presents you as an expert in your field," Samantha says.

For example, a social media manager can offer a class on how to increase engagement on your Facebook business page. You can announce your class on your website and all of your social media pages. Potential clients will be impressed that you are teaching others how to do what you do. That may cause a potential client to choose you over another social media manager. You have the opportunity to show those who sign up for your class all of the amazing services that you offer and potentially turn them into a client.

If you are interested in teaching online but are not sure what in the world you would teach, just take a look at your passions, hobbies, and job experience. A quick Google search for online classes will show you that there are online classes for just about every interest imaginable. Your job is to either find something in demand or put a unique spin on a class idea that has proven popular. Think about a common problem that many people want to solve. Could you create a class about it?

If you want to teach an online class or want to become a coach or consultant, I highly recommend Donna Partow's Take Your Message to the World class:

https://tv.donnapartow.net/take-your-message

or https://donnapartow.samcart.com/referral/E0gMt73h/SO7ziW3ryIPbQoiQ

The class is from a Christian perspective, but may be beneficial to anyone who wants to teach online.

Udemy (www.Udemy.com) offers training to help you create and host your own online class and market it to the world. It is a great platform to get started on because you will be able to offer your classes to their very large audience. They offer the option to upload videos of you teaching the material. Video classes are extremely popular and simple to create.

If you choose a topic that you are passionate about, it is very easy to simply record yourself talking about your passion for a few minutes.

Your students can take your classes at their own pace and contact you with any questions.

Here are some links to get you started:

https://www.udemy.com/teaching/

https://www.thepennyhoarder.com/make-money/how-to-create-online-courses/

Part Two: Getting Organized While Working At Home

Organize Your Home Office

The following section is designed to help you get the best start in your work-at-home career. You'll learn how to get your business setup correctly, organize your home office space, and keep good records. While much of this information focuses on running a home business, a lot of it applies to work-at-home employees as well.

After a few years of working from home, I found that I am definitely more organized when I have a separate space in my home for my business. If you don't have a spare room, even setting aside a corner of a room for a small desk and a filing cabinet can help you to be more organized and efficient.

You may also be able to write off a certain portion of your housing expenses (utilities, Internet, phone, etc.) if you can demonstrate that part of your home is used for business. Consult a tax professional on how to file your deductions properly.

Home Office Essentials

A reliable laptop is probably the most essential piece of equipment to any home office. While most business owners do just fine with a desktop, you may want to consider a laptop so that you can take work with you to a coffee shop or on a long road trip. If you will be visiting clients outside of your office, a laptop is essential.

Chances are you already own a computer. Make sure that it is running properly; otherwise, you will waste precious time and money waiting for a slow computer to load. If your computer is not reliable, investing in a newer model will save you time and money in the long run. Make sure that you are running a good anti-virus software on your computer.

Backup System

Losing important client work, records, or other business data because your computer crashed is a nightmare. You can purchase an external hard drive from any home office store for less than $100. This is money well spent when you consider how expensive data recovery services are.

I also recommend Carbonite, which automatically backs up your files. I once lost half a book I wrote and had to rewrite the entire thing. If I had had Carbonite, they would have been able to restore it for me. There are several similar cloud backup systems available, but this is the one my father-in-law uses for his business, and I've been using it ever since he recommended it to me. I never remember to back up my files manually, so this gives me peace of mind.

Carbonite: https://www.carbonite.com/

Here are some other ones I recommend:

Blackblaze (free trial): https://www.backblaze.com/cloud-backup.html#af9ppx

iDrive: https://www.idrive.com/p=ashleyemma

Take a few minutes to back up all of your important data on a regular basis or get a system to do it for you. Trust me, if anything ever happens to your computer, you will be so thankful that you took the extra time or made the small investment.

Printer and Scanner

Not every business requires a printer and scanner, but most businesses will need to print something once in a while. If you are on a limited budget and your business does not require you to print very often, you can probably get away with buying a basic printer. If your business requires you to print and scan records on a regular basis, invest in a high-quality printer/scanner. You can often find good deals online for quality computer ink and paper if you are willing to buy in bulk.

Filing System

Some form of both physical and electronic records are essential to any business. The more organized you are, the easier tax time will be for you. Keeping good client records can also save you a lot of time when that client that you haven't worked with in six months contacts you for another job.

Your filing system will depend largely upon what kind of business you operate. If all of your work is delivered electronically, it makes sense to keep an electronic file folder on each client that contains copies of all of the work that you have completed for that client and the related invoices.

If your business deals with physical products and paper receipts, you may want to keep a paper filing system. You can also scan in receipts to keep electronic copies of everything in case something ever happened to your physical records.

At the very least, you should keep records of:

- Every client and their contact information
- All invoices and customer receipts

- All receipts related to business expenses
- Legal documents related to your business (DBA certificate, tax id number, business license, etc.)
- Financial reports
- Previous year's tax returns and quarterly tax payments
- Any employee information
- Any other paperwork that is specific to your business

Whether you choose an electronic filing system, a traditional filing cabinet with hanging file folders or some combination of the two, it's important to find the system that works best for you.

Your Work Space

Just like your filing system, your work space depends on how you do business best. If your business requires you to meet with clients outside of the office all day, you may not need more than a corner of your dining table and your laptop. If you will be spending many hours a day in your home office, you want to make your work space inviting, comfortable, and efficient.

At minimum, invest in a sturdy desk with enough storage to meet your needs and the most comfortable chair that you can afford. Nothing makes it harder to work at a desk for long periods of time than a sore back.

If at all possible, set up your work space near a natural source of light. This increases productivity and just makes you feel better about sitting at a desk all day. Plan for a backup source of light for cloudy days.

Other Essentials

Consider your day-to-day routine and what you will need to make it run smoothly.

- Storage cabinets or bins
- A large worktable
- An oversized filing cabinet
- A large bookshelf
- Pictures of your family to remind you why you work so hard

Design your office or workspace to fit your specific business needs. If you can't purchase everything you need up front (most newbie entrepreneurs have limited budgets) make a list of tems to buy in the future and add to your office space as you can. Prioritize what you absolutely need to buy to run your business and buy what you can when your business starts taking off.

Setting Up Your Business Properly

By Nichole Cruz

This section on setting up your business is most beneficial for people who live in the United States. If you live outside of the U.S., please contact your local government offices to find out what laws and regulations apply to your business.

If you live in the U.S., this section is meant to give you a brief overview on how to set up your business properly.

Disclaimer: This section is meant to be used as a guideline and not specific legal advice. I am not a lawyer or accountant. It is important to research the business and tax laws in your city and state. Contact a tax professional and local government offices for specific advice.

Choosing a Business Structure

If you are self-employed and working under your legal name, you most likely won't need to worry about business structures or registering a business license. Your business is automatically considered a sole proprietorship.

Depending on what kind of business you run, you can choose to register your business as a limited liability corporation, partnership, or corporation. The structure that you choose will determine how much in taxes you will pay and what kind of liability protection you will have.

The Small Business Association's website provides a very easy to understand explanation on the pros and cons of each business structure:

https://www.sba.gov/business-guide/launch/choose-business-structure-types-chart

Do I Need to Register My Business?

According to the SBA's website, if you are operating your business under your legal name, you don't need to register your business. Otherwise, filing your fictitious business name with city and state agencies is often all that you need to do to register your business.

Your best bet is to talk with your local Small Business Association or county licensing office to find out exactly what you need to file for your specific business.

Self-employment Taxes and Business Taxes

According to www.irs.gov, if you make over $400 a year, you will need to pay self-employment taxes as a part of your personal tax return. Check out: https://www.irs.gov/businesses/small-businesses-self-employed/self-employment-tax-social-security-and-medicare-taxes

Typically, you should pay estimated taxes to the federal government once a quarter. Don't forget to set aside a portion of all of your business income for taxes. You don't ever want to be stuck with a burdensome tax bill that you can't pay.

If you choose to register your business as a partnership or corporation, you will need to file a separate tax return for your business.

One of the biggest financial benefits to being self-employed is the tax write-offs. You can write off most business expenses, mileage, and even a portion of your household expenses when you work from home. Be sure to save all of your receipts and document all of your expenses in order to take advantage of every write-off possible. A good CPA or accountant will help you take advantage of every deduction and file your tax returns properly. There are also many non-CPA professionals who are also competent and qualified to prepare taxes.

Take some time to get familiar with your state and federal business tax regulations. Even if you hire your own CPA or accountant to handle all of your taxes, you should at least be up to speed on the basic tax regulations. Remember you are the boss, so it is ultimately your responsibility to make sure that your business is in order.

Visit the following link to learn more:

https://www.irs.gov/businesses/small-businesses-self-employed/business-taxes

Employment Identification Number (EIN)

An EIN is like a social security number for your business. You'll need one in order to pay federal taxes, hire employees, open a business bank account, and apply for business licenses and permits. I personally think that everyone who operates any kind of business should apply for an EIN instead of using your social security number. This keeps your social security number safer and you'll be able to open a business bank account. A business bank account makes it so much easier to track business income and expenses. Merging business and personal accounts often leads to costly mistakes. Why risk it?

It's simple and free to apply for an Employer Identification Number on www.irs.gov.

Keep Your Finances in Order from Day One

With everything that you need to do to get your business up and running, it may be tempting to put off getting your finances in order until you start making some serious income. Don't put this off. Make it easy on yourself by following a few simple steps to stay organized from the start:

1. Keep your business and personal finances completely separate from one another from day one. Having to sort through your personal checking account for business expenses at tax

time is a huge pain. Shop around for a low-fee checking and savings account.

2. Make a plan for your business income. Come up with a financial plan that includes all of your expected expenses (including your salary), tax money, and savings that you will invest to grow your business. Stick to the budget and plan for unexpected expenses.

3. Write yourself a paycheck. When you work for yourself, it is too easy to either underpay yourself when you want to grow your business, or overspend when you should be investing more in your business. It is important to decide on a salary for yourself and stick to it so that your business and personal finances stay as separate as possible.

4. Track every dollar that you make and spend every month. If you take a few minutes at the end of your business day to track any money you made and spent that day, it will be painless. The last thing that you want to do is have to spend hours sifting through old receipts and invoices in order to get your financial records up to date. This will also make tax season much easier.

5. Make a budget. Once you do start to make good money, you might be tempted to spend it. You might not realize you're spending more than you should, and at the end of the month you'll wonder where all the money you made went. Been there, done that, and it still happens. You might hate the idea of budgeting, or maybe you tried it before and didn't stick with it long. I recently discovered this simple budgeting strategy by Jordan Page, and it changed my perspective on budgeting.

Check out Jordan's simple budgeting technique on YouTube:
https://www.youtube.com/watch?v=VCr-54OH7IY

Ashley's Legit Work-at-Home Jobs Productivity (

✓ Get out of the house as much as you can. You could do your work at a library so you're not distracted by chores, napping, or TV.

✓ Check online to see if there is a work-at-home group in your local area that you can join, or join a Facebook group. This support group will help you tremendously. It will help to talk to other people who also work at home and understand your struggles and successes, especially if no one else you know works from home. You can encourage each other.

✓ Exercise each morning before work.

✓ If you can, keep your phone on airplane mode or on silent while you're working so you're not distracted by texts, phone calls, and Facebook notifications. Every time your phone makes a noise it can totally wreck your train of thought or make you lose your place. If you get business calls or messages on your phone, then you might not be able to do this for too long. For example, when I have a good 30-minute or one-hour time block where I can really focus on my work, I put my phone on silent and return any calls or emails after. Or you can use the app called Forest which will help you not touch your phone while you work by growing a little tree on your screen: https://www.forestapp.cc/en/.

✓ Try using a filter or social media restricting app on your browser to help you concentrate on real work. This way you won't be distracted by Facebook or funny cat videos on YouTube. You might only intend to spend five minutes on sites like this, which can easily turn into an hour. Try out the app for your browser called Cold Turkey: https://getcoldturkey.com/.

✓ When people find out you're working at home, some will think that you don't do much all day or can stop working whenever you want. Don't be surprised if people start to drop by unannounced, thinking you have time during the day to hang out. Politely let them know that you are working, and you won't be finished until the time that you have scheduled. Your job is just like a traditional job in the sense that you can't take time to talk with someone or be interrupted by an unexpected visitor.

✓ If you need help staying focused, listen to white noise or nature sounds. Some people like to play music while working, which might work for you, but it distracts me personally unless there are no lyrics. Classical music might work for you or other types of music with no lyrics.

multitask. Don't think you can watch TV and work at the same time, even if you're doing simple work. It'll probably take you twice as long.

Have an organized filing system and keep your files up to date. Make sure everything is documented and filed properly, and keep your tax paperwork handy in a fireproof metal filing cabinet.

- ✓ Keep track of your income and expenses on a daily and monthly basis so you have less work to do during tax season.

- ✓ Bookkeeping and taxes should be your number one priority. Paperwork is probably what I am worst at, but it needs to be top priority. Every receipt should be documented and filed in a timely manner. If you don't know how, hire someone experienced. It will save you time and money in the long run. Hire a qualified professional for your tax preparation and use software like Quickbooks (www.quickbooks.com) to help you stay organized.

- ✓ Try to pay for expenses with the same system you use for when your clients pay you. For example, because I mostly use Paypal to get paid, so I use Paypal to pay for my clients' book marketing, editing, etc. It makes it much easier to keep track of and add up for taxes because it is all in one place. I occasionally also have clients who pay me with credit cards, but it still is much easier than using several different payment methods. This won't work for everyone, but it works well for me.

- ✓ Don't get so busy working at home that you let your home life suffer. Take some time for yourself every day. Play with your kids, hang out with your spouse or partner, read a book, or go out with friends. Remember to have fun sometimes.

- ✓ Set very clear, specific goals. For example, set a goal for making $5,000 in March or get 2 new clients in the next 2 weeks. Write it down, and put it somewhere you will see it every day, like on your desk.

- ✓ Create an office space that is separate from your sleeping and relaxing area, no matter how small.

- ✓ Set work hours and stick to them.

- ✓ Wake up at the same time every morning and maintain a routine like you would with an office job.

- ✓ Waking up early might be the hardest part of working from home. It's so tempting to sleep in with no one to keep you accountable. My baby wakes me up early to eat, so I try to get started on my work right after instead of going back to bed. This way I can get at least an hour of work done before my toddler wakes up. To be honest, this doesn't always happen. Sometimes I do go back to bed if I've been up a lot with the baby that night, and that's ok because I can make up for it later in the day. However, I definitely get the most work done on days where I get to work right away early in the morning.

- ✓ Dozens of studies show that waking up early in the morning turns you into a more proactive person, resulting in more productivity.

- ✓ Always get dressed, even if it's in comfortable clothes. Don't wear your PJs. If you like to do your hair or wear makeup when you normally go out, then do that as well. It doesn't matter if no one else sees you. It totally changes your mindset. Most days someone does drop by my house, even for a moment, so it is good to always look presentable. Dr. Karen Pine, professor of psychology at the University of Hertfordshire, says, "When we put on an item of clothing it is common for the wearer to adopt the characteristics associated with that garment. A lot of clothing has symbolic meaning for us, whether it's 'professional work attire' or 'relaxing weekend wear,' so when we put it on, we prime the brain to behave in ways consistent with that meaning."

- ✓ Make your bed every morning. Many of the most successful and productive people in the world make their beds every day.

- ✓ Every night before you go to bed, look at your calendar and to write a list for the next day. Write down anything you can think of that you need to add to your to do list so your mind is clear and you can sleep better.

- ✓ When it looks like you're going to have a good month, don't get complacent. Line up as much work as you can and start scheduling work in weeks or months in advance as you get busier.

- ✓ Stock up on and organize your desk supplies. Know where everything is so you don't have to look for it every time you need a fresh pencil, pen or notepad.

- ✓ Get the best ergonomically correct desk chair you can afford to prevent back problems and other health issues.

- ✓ Keep your desk organized and decorated beautifully so you enjoy working there. Don't feel guilty for investing some money in some new dry erase boards, picture frames, pen holders, desk organizers, wall art, etc. If your desk is lovely to look at, you'll be happier working there.

- ✓ Have water, tissues, lip balm, pens, paper, or other things you use often right in your reach where you are working so you aren't constantly getting up to get them. While it is good to get up and move around, you might get distracted and sidetracked while looking for things.

- ✓ Don't forget to eat healthy meals, no matter how busy you get.

- ✓ Create a schedule of how you want your day to look. For example, start work every day at

8:00 and have pre-scheduled breaks throughout the day for lunch, working out, etc. With little kids at home, I can't stick to a strict schedule, but I do have a routine. For example, I work early in the morning, whenever my kids nap, and at night after my husband gets home. When my kids are awake, I do housework and spend time with them.

- ✓ Remember to step away from your computer often. It's not healthy to sit for long periods of time. Go out and walk around as much as you can, run on the treadmill, or do some jumping jacks or burpees in your living room. You'll find it refreshing and that it gives you more energy for the rest of the day.

- ✓ Stand up often. If you feel tired, standing or stretching can help wake you up. I have noticed that I can feel sleepy after sitting in one place for too long, but once I get moving, my energy comes back. Sometimes I stand and work on my laptop at the kitchen counter. You can also try moving from your desk to the table, or work outside if it's nice out. A change of environment can make a huge difference.

- ✓ Enjoy the experience, and be thankful that you get to work at home—something many people dream of. If you're doing what you love, you won't give up when it gets hard.

- ✓ Block time at the end of the week to wrap up loose ends, get small tasks done, and plan for the following week.

- ✓ Physical planner books are great, but I also highly recommend using Evernote on your phone to have a to-do list that is on you at all times. When you think of something that needs to be done, you can add it to your to do list before you forget. I don't know what I would do without Evernote. I have dozens of "notebooks" and lists on there, but I use my To Do List the most. Use this link to get one month of the Premium version for free, or you can use the Basic free version: (https://www.evernote.com/ or https://www.evernote.com/referral/Registration.action?sig=311fcbeb27721cc4313f7ff4f0 3963f9c9528533bd36b352fff54fb57f15a97b&uid=48690587)

- ✓ Take weekends off whenever you can. I am so guilty of working six or seven days a week, but lately I've been really trying hard to take weekends off, even if I have to do extra work on Fridays. Taking time off and not overworking will preserve your mental and physical health, and that will be much more beneficial in the long run.

- ✓ You will make mistakes in the beginning, and you won't have all the kinks worked out right away, and this is okay. Learn from your mistakes, make a note, and don't make them again. As time passes, you will get faster and better at what you do.

- ✓ Schedule time for your work, but also your health, fun, friends and family, etc. If you don't, you will find that very quickly your time is completely taken over by work.

- ✓ Every now and then, not counting weekends, take a scheduled day off. This can be a day

you can do something you love, like go to the beach or out to lunch with a friend, or you might need to use it for errands or chores. Don't let yourself do any work. This will help you clear your head and will help your work performance long-term.

✓ As soon as you get busy enough, raise your prices to prevent over working yourself. People will also take you more seriously and see more value in what you do. Don't be afraid to raise your rates! Charge what you're worth.

✓ Don't give up even when you feel discouraged. It will get difficult—that is a guarantee. If working from home were easy, everyone would do it. While it does have huge rewards, it also has massive challenges. Get through the tough times, like when a client is unhappy with your work or you have a very slow month, and you'll be so glad you persevered when your business flourishes and you're making bank.

✓ If you don't have an office, try to make one if you can find the space. You don't need much space, just enough room for a desk is probably enough. I recently made an office out of a utility closet in my basement. With a desk, nice décor, and a space heater, it's really inviting and I love working in there.

Work at Home Jobs Links List

Legit Jobs for Companies:

Leap Force

http://www.leapforce.com

Appen

https://join.appen.com/

Writers Domain

http://www.writersdomain.net

Rev

https://www.rev.com/freelancers/captions

VIP Desk

https://vipdeskconnect.com/current-openings/

Convergys

http://www.convergys.com

Freelance Websites:

Fiverr (I personally use Fiverr and am most familiar with it)

http://www.fiverr.com

https://www.fiverr.com/russ41burg/show-you-how-to-become-a-top-fiverr-seller

Upwork

http://www.upwork.com

Thumbtack

http://www.thumbtack.com

Freelancer

http://www.freelancer.com

Online Classes:

Donna Partow's Take Your Message to the World class (for coaches, online teachers, consultants and experts):

https://tv.donnapartow.net/take-your-message or

https://donnapartow.samcart.com/referral/E0gMt73h/SO7ziW3ryIPbQoiQ

For Gina Horkey's Virtual Assistant and Freelance Writing online courses, just go to www.horkeyhandbook.com or use my affiliate links below:

30 Days or Less to Freelance Writing Success Course:

https://horkeyhandbook.samcart.com/referral/30-Days-or-Less-to-Freelance-Writing-Success/RO7AGdsWbyYJMdKj

Free "How to Become a Freelance Writer" Blogpost:

https://horkeyhandbook.samcart.com/how-to-become-a-paid-freelance-writer

Not sure what writing niche to specialize in?

https://horkeyhandbook.samcart.com/referral/freelance-writing-niches/RO7AGdsWbyYJMdKj

Gina Horkey's 30 Days or Less to Virtual Assistant Success Course:

https://horkeyhandbook.samcart.com/referral/30-Days-or-Less-to-Virtual-Assistant-Success-Sales-Page/RO7AGdsWbyYJMdKj

Free "How to Become a Virtual Assistant" Blogpost:

https://horkeyhandbook.samcart.com/referral/how-to-become-a-virtual-assistant/RO7AGdsWbyYJMdKj

Not sure what services to offer as a new Virtual Assistant?

https://horkeyhandbook.samcart.com/referral/va-services-list/RO7AGdsWbyYJMdKj

Check out Gina's site:

www.horkeyhandbook.com

https://horkeyhandbook.com/?sc_ref=RO7AGdsWbyYJMdKj

VA finder:

https://horkeyhandbook.samcart.com/referral/2aIdgwUw/RO7AGdsWbyYJMdKj

Success Stories:

https://horkeyhandbook.samcart.com/referral/sss/RO7AGdsWbyYJMdKj

Christian PEN (Freelance writing and editing classes)

https://thechristianpen.com/

https://peninstitute.com/

Caitlin Pyle's Proofread Anywhere course (Legal transcript proofreading course)

https://caitlinpyle.com/pa

https://proofreadanywhere.com/work-at-home-job-ideas-for-detail-oriented-people/

Caitlin Pyle's free webinar on general proofreading:

https://learn.proofreadanywhere.com/automated-webinar-funnel-template?affiliate_id=690241

Proofreading Mini Course

https://caitlinpyle.com/optin

Internet Scoping School

https://scopeschool.com/ashleyemma/1

Amazon FBA and The Selling Family (Amazon FBA business)

https://thesellingfamily.com

Writing Books, Publishing, and Ghostwriting

Self-Publishing School's free workshop: How to Go from Blank Page to Bestseller in 90 Days:

https://xe172.isrefer.com/go/sps4fta-vts/ashleyemma1

KDP Rocket: https://jvz9.com/c/843169/225041

KDROI: https://jvz4.com/c/843169/179288 or https://www.kdroi.com/

KDSpy: https://jvz5.com/c/843169/111047 or https://www.kdspy.com

BookAds: http://bookads.co/?ref=amishbookwriter@gmail.com or www.bookads.com

Free course on Amazon ads: https://kindlepreneur.com/ams-book-advertising-course/

ISBNs from Bowker

www.bowker.com

KDP Rocket (best book marketing tool ever): www.kdprocket.com or https://jvz9.com/c/843169/225041

Agent Resources

http://pred-ed.com/

http://www.writersdigest.com/

http://absolutewrite.com/forums/activity.php?s=d48daa01e0f78dfb53075491f65a8207

http://www.publishersmarketplace.com/

Kathy Ide (an excellent editor who specializes in query letters)

www.KathyIde.com

Authors Publish Magazine (sign up for their valuable newsletters about publishers seeking manuscripts)

https://www.authorspublish.com/

support@authorspublish.com

The 2017 Guide to Manuscript Publishers: https://www.amazon.com/2017-Guide-Manuscript-Publishers-Traditional-ebook/dp/B073HQJPVS

https://www.authorspublish.com/submit-to-authors-publish-magazine/

Fearless Author

http://a.co/5IqzNDR

High Performance Paperback

http://a.co/hZPKoR1

Ghostwriting Resources

http://associationofghostwriters.org/ - Sign up for the free eBook on how to find ghostwriting gigs

https://thewritelife.com/how-to-become-a-ghostwriter/

Self-Publishing Article

https://proofreadanywhere.com/3-reasons-you-should-consider-self-publishing-a-book-and-how-to-get-started/

Proofreading, Editing, and Scoping

(See Proofread Anywhere info above)

Scoping School's free mini-course:

https://scopeschool.com/ashleyemma/1

Grammar Blogs to Follow

Daily Grammar

http://www.dailygrammar.com

Grammarist

http://www.grammarist.com

Grammar Girl

http://www.quickanddirtytips.com/grammar-girl.

Margie Wakeman Wells (Resources for grammar for proofreading legal transcripts)

http://www.margieholdscourt.com

Christian Editor Connection

https://christianeditor.com/editors/

Blogging

Web Hosting: Bluehost

http://www.bluehost.com

Web Hosting: Hostgator

http://www.hostgator.com

Money Saving Mom (Blogging class)

http://moneysavingmom.com/about

Blogelina (Blogging class and helpful articles)

http://www.blogelina.com

http://blogelina.com/how-to-start-your-own-profitable-blog

Smart Blogger

https://smartblogger.com/start-here/

Wedding work:

Wedding Wire

www.weddingwire.com

Building your Website:

Wix

http://wixstats.com/?a=16616&c=2252&s1=

Wordpress

https://wordpress.com/

Social Media Manager Resources:

Social Monkey Business' free online class: "How To be a Successful, Highly Paid Social Media

Manager":

https://socialmonkeybusiness.com/special-webinar-event

http://socialmarketingwriting.com/complete-guide-successful-social-media-manager/

http://www.socialmediatoday.com/content/9-steps-starting-out-social-media-manager

Direct Sales Resources:

http://directsellingnews.com/index.php/view/dsn_announces_the_2017_global_100#.Wd-ORWhSzIU

https://www.moneymakingmommy.com/direct-sales-company-list-2011/

Making and Selling Cakes or Other Types of Food:

Check with your local government to make sure that you have all necessary licenses and permits: https://www.sba.gov/blogs/so-youd-start-home-based-baking-business-now-what

Teaching Classes Online

Donna Partow's Take Your Message to the World class (for coaches, online teachers, consultants and experts):

https://tv.donnapartow.net/take-your-message

or https://donnapartow.samcart.com/referral/E0gMt73h/SO7ziW3ryIPbQoiQ

More information on how to land a remote teaching gig

https://www.teachaway.com/online-teaching-jobs

More resources

https://www.udemy.com/teaching/

https://www.thepennyhoarder.com/make-money/how-to-create-online-courses/

Payment Websites:

www.PayPal.com

www.Stripe.com

www.Moneygram.com

www.Payoneer.com

Setting Up Your Business:

www.irs.gov

https://www.irs.gov/businesses/small-businesses-self-employed/self-employment-tax-social-security-and-medicare-taxes

https://www.irs.gov/businesses/small-businesses-self-employed/business-taxes

https://www.sba.gov/business-guide/launch/choose-business-structure-types-chart

Simple Budgeting Technique Video

https://www.youtube.com/watch?v=VCr-54OH7IY

Carbonite

www.carbonite.com

Blackblaze (free trial)

https://www.backblaze.com/cloud-backup.html#af9ppx

iDrive

https://www.idrive.com/p=ashleyemma

Quickbooks

www.quickbooks.com

Other helpful links:

Glass Door

https://www.glassdoor.com/index.htm

Forest App

https://www.forestapp.cc/en/

Cold Turkey App

https://getcoldturkey.com/

Work-At-Home Moms

www.wahm.com

ScheduleOnce

https://www.scheduleonce.com/pricing?refcode=AEP818

KDP Rocket (effective book marketing tool)

https://jvz9.com/c/843169/225041

Question and Answer Site

www.Quora.com

Evernote (Click below to get a month free of the Premium version, or you can use the free Basic version.)

www.evernote.com
(https://www.evernote.com/referral/Registration.action?sig=311fcbeb27721cc4313f7ff4f03963f9c9528533bd36b352fff54fb57f15a97b&uid=48690587)

Monster

www.Monster.com

Udemy

www.Udemy.com

Ashley's Links:

Ashley's Salon Wedding Wire Profile to use as an example

https://www.weddingwire.com/biz/ashleys-salon-biddeford/cdb5095e4f9071ab.html

Ashley's Salon Facebook Page to use as an example

https://www.facebook.com/ashleyssalonbiddeford/

Ashley's Author and Fearless Publishing House Website

www.ashleyemmaauthor.com

Schedule a free strategy session with me personally if you have questions about self-publishing or starting your own publishing company. I'd be happy to point you in the right direction or give you feedback on your Amazon eBook listing page. Contact me at ashley@ashleyemmaauthor.com.

Bonus Section: Real Stories From Work-At-Home Professionals

There are so many ways to make a living from home. As you learned in Part One of this book, I had several flops and failures before I found a few niches that worked for me. But what worked for me may not be the right fit for you. I asked a few of my friends who have started successful work-at-home ventures to share their stories with you. I hope that you will find their stories inspiring as you begin exploring the right home career or business for you.

Oksana's Story

Health coach

My twin sister Viktoriya and I were raised in Ukraine in Eastern Europe (next to Russia).

My parents got married very young and we (five of us – our brother, mom, dad, and us) grew up living in a one-bedroom apartment in Kharkov, Ukraine. Our apartment only had 1 small bedroom, kitchen, and bathroom. Our mother was a midwife and she often worked 24-hour shifts delivering babies. One time, she delivered 26 babies in 24 hours. Our dad was one of the top engineers in the company he worked for.

However, the money was tight. Our dad was often paid with food (such as cases of apple juice and sausages) and due to the financial struggles and other stresses, he had a heart attack at 30 years old. Because the ambulance took a long time to get to us, our mom had to act fast, and she saved his life by giving him an epi shot.

A year later, our dad was attacked in the subway on his way home from work by a gang who beat him up to the point of unrecognition and robbed him. Somehow, he found his way home and our mom, again, helped him get better.

Our parents made $10,000 US dollars per year, but because our grandparents had their own farm, we always had food on the table.

When we were 12 years old, our dad got an amazing opportunity to work as an engineer in Michigan. He took this offer despite not knowing a word of English, not having a driver's license, no bank account, and only $300 in his pocket. In one year, he learned English (by studying hard every night after work) and they offered him a permanent job.

When we came to the US, we started eating a standard American diet, and years into this diet we started getting symptoms of cystic acne, chronic migraines, sore throat infections, and unwanted weight gain.

While in high school, I (Oksana) started volunteering in a cancer research lab and continued working there throughout college. Together, Viktoriya and I studied nutrition and health coaching and

continued our outside training with various doctors and physicians.

Running a business and having another full-time job is of course very challenging. You must have a strong mindset and be passionate about what you do. We work 18-hour days, and if we weren't passionate about our health coaching, it would be difficult to stay sane! In between my research, I troubleshoot website issues, deal with spammers, malware, set up webinars, funnels, answer emails, and book appointments. My twin sister Viktoriya focuses on marketing and being the best coach for our clients. She also works as an animator on a kid's TV show in California.

It's very important to find and build a master-mind alliance, because when you surround yourself with people who have similar dreams and goals, it makes you level up.

This is the advice that we would give to entrepreneurs and those who are interested in starting their own business:

1) "Never give up." -Winston Churchill

2) Leaders are readers. Learning is probably the most important currency you can have.

3) Build a vision wall and write down your short-term and long-term goals, and work towards them every day.

4) Celebrate your wins and accomplishments.

5) When you can't find a good companion to walk with, it's better to be alone than to be with those who will hinder your progress.

6) While your time and your labor may be subject to the demands of your employer and others, your mind is the one thing that cannot be controlled by anyone but you. The thoughts you think, your attitude toward your job, and what you are willing to give in exchange for the compensation you are paid are entirely up to you. Only you can determine whether you will be a slave to a negative attitude or the master of a positive one. Your attitude, your only master in life, is entirely within your control. When you control your attitude toward events, you control the eventual implication of those events.

7) "You were born to win, but to be a winner, you must plan to win, prepare to win, and expect to win." -Zig Ziglar

8) As Zig Ziglar also said, "Failure is an event, not a person. Success or a win doesn't make you, and a failure or loss doesn't break you."

9) You must look back in forgiveness, forward in hope, down in compassion and up in gratitude.

10) Be decisive, deputize, supervise, and do things in the order of their importance.

11) Do your best, forget the rest.

12) Be honest, sincere, and authentic.

13) Focus on your own progress and don't worry what other people are doing.

Best,

Oksana Gruzdyn

Health Coaches and Nutritionist

PhD Candidate in Immunology

http://viktoriyaandoksana.com/

https://www.instagram.com/viktoriyaandoksana/

viktoriyaandoksana@gmail.com

Kevin's Story: Working from Home Can Still Be a Calling

Bestselling author and coach

When I was a child, the holiday season seemed so magical. Almost every December the Connecticut landscape was coated with a few inches or more of fresh white snow. I remember my father plowing the grounds of his boss's estate on what seemed to be the biggest plow in the world at that time. My older brother and I would build snow forts and snowmen and have snowball fights with the kids in the neighborhood. By the time we had enough winter sport for the day, we were all soaked through to the skin.

My father was the superintendent of an estate and my mom was a stay-at-home housewife. I was the youngest of three children, my brother was three years older, and my sister was eight years older. I don't know how my father could afford to support a family of five on the meager salary he made back then. Somehow, he always provided everything we needed and then some. He didn't say much. He worked hard and left the discipline to Mom. After a hard day of work, he liked to eat dinner and then put his feet up and watch his TV programs.

Mom kept the house in pristine order. Every inch of our house was sparkling, fresh, and clean. Every night would be a delicious homemade meal with the whole family at the dinner table.

Our clothes were always clean, folded, ironed, and put away in our rooms. She was truly an amazing woman.

It was a magical time in my life, maybe the best time in some ways. I know I will always have wonderful memories of my childhood in Connecticut.

My father took a leap of faith and started his own construction business. He moved the whole family into the center of town, a low-income area. Keep in mind the town we lived in was a very wealthy town. It had to be very difficult for my parents to keep up with the local prices. Again, somehow my father managed to take care of all of the family's needs. I'm still amazed at his commitment.

If I wanted to get a college degree, it was up to me. There would be no going away to college and partying the semester away with the parents paying for everything.

I have always been a worker ever since I was fifteen years old. I have a very diverse background that started as a construction worker with my father, then a bouncer and bartender. I've done several types of jobs ranging from a restaurant manager to a licensed and ordained reverend.

Now I'm the multi-bestselling author of over thirty books, and I'm also a Christian coach for those who suffer from addictions. I earned my Ph.D., and I also have many certifications, licenses, and degrees earned before my Ph.D.

Everything in my life was going quite well. I was earning a great living, doing what I wanted to do, traveling, having a wonderful time.

Then, one day my life drastically changed. My right hip started to feel stiff and painful and quickly became worse. The surgeon told me that there was nothing they could do for me except a full hip replacement after I lost more than fifty percent of my body weight.

I was a super-heavyweight powerlifter. Then some time later my left shoulder was also worn out and full of arthritis.

I was in a wheelchair within a few months.

I had to find a way that I could work from home to be able to supplement my income and survive. I already knew that I was a pretty good writer and teacher from working at the ministry for many years. I started teaching for an online school for professionals which I could do from my home computer. I also kept writing articles, essays, books, and I became better at the craft. I read books on writing and watched how-to videos.

I would contact different websites and publications to ask if I could submit articles. It was slow going at first, but now they contact me to write articles for their publications, blogs, and websites. I've done numerous radio interviews and some television appearances.

I have thousands of published articles and over thirty published books, most have made the Amazon Top 100 Best-Seller List!

I also took a ton of free webinars to learn as much as I could. To make money as a writer and author, you must establish yourself as an expert in whatever niche you choose. I was fortunate to already be an expert in a few niches. You need to identify who your customer is, who you are writing for, and figure out your authentic voice in writing.

To be an author you also have to be a marketer or hire a good one. Once you have a book published on a subject, your credibility as an expert increases. Some people then sell other products like video courses and training, live events, etc.

I love to teach, and I love to write! I'm an expert on addiction recovery and also on professional coaching. You could also say that I'm an expert on weight training since I was a two-time World Bench Press Champion and won several other weight lifting competitions.

I have already helped thousands of individuals and their families to overcome addiction problems, and I have trained hundreds of professionals in the addiction treatment and coaching industries. I just need to continue to get the word out about my books and self-improvement journals.

I haven't gotten rich yet by any means; however, I believe that in the long run, I will be able to live more comfortably. Writing also keeps me busy, which is a good thing, being in a wheelchair; I don't know what I would do if I wasn't a writer. I don't teach online at the school any longer.

I also ghostwrite and help other people to get their first book published. I help people with content for their websites, blogs, etc. I make videos, power-point presentations, book covers and videos. I'm a nationally-certified interventionist and an internationally-certified addictions coach.

I think it's important to do a job that we love to do and that betters our world. If we can do that, we have been a success no matter what is in our bank account.

Rev. Dr. Kevin T. Coughlin Ph.D.

https://www.revkevsrecoveryworld.com/

Maria's Story

Proofreader and Virtual Assistant

I've always loved to read since I was very young. I was that student who was always in the school/city library, the bookmobile, and always got a free pizza for BOOK IT! For study hall, I signed up to work in the school library instead, and I'd get in trouble sometimes for reading during classes. As I grew up, I'd notice spelling and grammar errors in the books I'd read and other everyday places.

I'd always thought it would be great to get paid to read and find errors. It seemed like most of those types of jobs required some sort of degree, though. That is, until I found *Proofread Anywhere*.

I found out about the *Proofread Anywhere* course in early March 2015 and I signed up for the free 7-day intro course. Once I went through that, I realized that though I had a knack for finding errors, I needed more training when it came to proofreading for court reporters, so I signed up for the course right after that and finished at the end of May 2015.

The fact that I didn't need a degree to do this was a major factor in my decision to learn how to proofread transcripts. I had also been trying to find a way to make some extra income on the side since I do still have a day job. This seemed quite convenient because it wouldn't require me having to go to another physical location to work. Plus, it would be something I'd enjoy doing and wouldn't really seem like work. My hope is to eventually leave my day job and make proofreading one of a few freelancing jobs instead.

The most challenging part was finding the time to take the course with everything else I had going on. But because of the portability this job offers, I was able to find time to take the course at my own pace, and it was easier than I thought it would be.

I would say learning how to market myself was most valuable to me. I have never been good at sales in general. In the past, I'd signed up for a few direct sales companies, but I never really made any money. But the course teaches you how to market yourself and in more than one way -- and it worked! I no longer fear putting myself out there and reaching out to potential clients.

I have a court reporter friend, and she started sending me work once I finished the course. On my own, I was able to find my second client within a few days of finishing the course. I never thought I'd be able to take on clients while still having a day job, but it's worked out well so far. The nice thing is that I can always take on more clients as the need arises and my circumstances change, as they have recently.

For me, finding *Proofread Anywhere* has opened the door to other opportunities I wouldn't have considered before. In the two years I've been part-time proofreading, I've also added business proofreading. All of this has also led me to branch out into being a virtual assistant, not only as part of the Proofread Anywhere team but also assisting a few court reporters as well. And if that wasn't enough, I've also further branched out into virtual bookkeeping for a few amazing clients so far. It only made sense to do so since my day job is in accounting.

So now that I offer services as a freelance proofreader, virtual assistant, and virtual bookkeeper and have acquired a good clientele, I'm well on my way to eventually being my own boss. Once that happens, I know I'll be able to take on more clients. Who knows what else I may be able to add as a service? Really, the sky's the limit.

Maria Arellano

Professional proofreader

www.AnywhereVirtually.com

Articles on *Proofread Anywhere:*

http://www.businessinsider.com/caitlin-pyle-proofread-anywhere-2015-8

https://proofreadanywhere.com/work-at-home-job-ideas-for-detail-oriented-people/

Interested in general proofreading? Here's a free training:

https://learn.proofreadanywhere.com/automated-webinar-funnel-template?affiliate_id=690241

You can also try out a free mini-course on proofreading here: https://caitlinpyle.com/optin

A free 45-minute seminar to help prospective students determine whether or not a career in proofreading is right for them:

https://learn.proofreadanywhere.com/registergptpfb?affiliate_id=690241

Russel's Story

Fiverr.com entrepreneur expert

Fiverr is now one of the leading places for freelancers to find work in the online community. It provides the platform, the customers, lots of ideas and great support while you provide the ideas and services and do the work for those customers.

The basic way it works is that you create a profile with 'gigs' and when a customer buys a gig they pay a fee. This fee, in its most basic form, is often $5, but you can earn much more than that, depending on what you can do. There are some gigs that are thousands of dollars.

Sound simple? It is. I have been working through Fiverr for over two years now and my monthly earnings, after Fiverr takes their cut, have hit around $4000. I could do more, but I still have something of a life and $4000 represents enough income for me to live well.

I had a recent order for over $1000 and have had ones at $500 and $700. I've had offers to do jobs for more than that and some that come somewhere in between.

So, what type of gigs can you do? The answer to that is almost anything, so long as it's legal. Creative writing is my thing, but advertising, graphics, business plans, resumes and a thousand other things are sold by thousands of sellers every day.

The best gigs are the ones you can complete fast. If you can think of something that lots of people want and you can produce it in 5 minutes, you could be on your way to earning $48 per hour. And if you can find something you can produce in half that time? You do the math.

But becoming a top seller on Fiverr doesn't happen overnight, or by accident. It takes a lot of knowledge, some skill, and a ton of patience to get to the stage where orders are arriving on a regular basis.

I made a lot of mistakes when I first came to the site. I didn't really know what I was doing, and to some extent, I am still learning today.

I stuck with it, I learned from my mistakes and now I work from home and have given up the day job.

Doesn't that sound great?

It does. Believe me. It's a great feeling getting up every morning and finding that I have plenty of work to do.

It's great knowing that I can work whenever I feel like it and then go to the gym, walk the dog, see friends or go on vacation.

My life no longer revolves around work. My work revolves around my life, and it feels a lot better for it.

And you could earn a significant income, or even your primary income, from Fiverr. By employing some basic and simple strategies, you can see your orders steadily increasing from monthly, to weekly, to daily and, quite possibly, to hourly.

It really is possible. My orders have gradually increased, both in number and value, over the time that I have been selling, and they show no signs of diminishing any time soon. There is simply a lot of demand.

There are also a lot of sellers on Fiverr, of course, and some of them are very good. But there are a lot of poor ones too. Often a product is not as described, of poor quality or simply not delivered. Some sellers see online work as something which is easy and will make them a living without any effort.

I'm going to tell you now, that isn't the case and if you want to become a top Fiverr seller with a strong approval rating, then you have to start strong and do your best.

So, take my advice. You need a great profile page, outstanding customer service and a willingness to go the extra mile for your customers, providing them with quality and value at the same time.

Here are some tips for success if you want to try offering your services on freelance sites like Fiverr:

1. Go with your passion. It may seem obvious, but if you do what you love rather than what you think will sell, you will be more likely to attract clients. Allow your passion to shine through on your profile.

2. Make a profile that attracts clients. When you sign up for any freelancer site, you will have the opportunity to create a profile that showcases your work, describes your services, and tells your client a bit about you. Take the time to fill out every section of the profile. Choose your best pieces of work to showcase if the profile allows for a portfolio of your work (most do). List all your relevant experience, and highlight the skills you think will be most important to a potential client. Ask a friend to proofread your profile to catch silly typos that will make you look unprofessional.

3. Learn from those who have had success. All of these websites have some form of blog, tutorial, or forum to learn how to make your profile stand out and get more sales. Take some time to glean from any resources that the website offers, and don't be afraid to ask questions on the forums. Many people who have been successful on these websites are willing to give you valuable advice.

4. Take a few lower paying jobs in the beginning. When you are starting out on a freelancing website, you want to get a few good reviews as quickly as possible. Good reviews show potential clients that you are great at what you do. The easiest way to get a few jobs under your belt is to bid on as many jobs as possible and offer a very low bid. Let the client know you are an experienced (insert your skill here), but you are new to this community and would like to offer a great deal in order to build up a few good reviews. Many people who come to these sites are looking for a good, cheap gig and will take you up on your offer.

5. Actively seek out jobs. Many freelancers make the mistake of simply putting up a profile or a website and expecting clients to come to them. Successful freelancers use any time that they are not working on gigs to find new clients. Bid on as many jobs as possible. Promote your offer on social media, Craigslist, forums, and any other place you can think of. Don't spam, or you might lose your account.

6. Don't work for peanuts once you get established. Once you have a few jobs under your belt, raise your rates to reflect what other top freelancers in your industry are charging on the freelancer website. Keep in mind that many people are coming to sites like Fiverr for cheap gigs, so you won't get many jobs if you price yourself too high. Play around with different rates until you find a rate that you are happy to make and still attract clients.

For those who are just starting out, I offer a gig which will get you going quickly and smoothly, offering you the chance to start earning in days, or even hours, not the weeks or months it takes for some.

You can find it by following the link here https://www.fiverr.com/russ41burg/show-you-how-to-become-a-top-fiverr-seller. I guarantee that if you follow the steps and advice I provide inside these pages, you will have recouped the trivial pittance you paid for the gig within the first week. And within a month you'll be wondering why you didn't take up this line of work sooner.

-Russel Burgess

Fiverr expert and author of *Traitor in the Reich*

Conclusion

I hope this book has helped you decide what type of work-at-home or online job you want to do so you can get started quickly. Working from home or anywhere you want in the world is such an exciting journey! I am thankful I was able to have a small part in your journey and share my struggles and tips for success with you so you can learn from them.

If this book helped you in any way, I'd love to hear about it! Feel free to email me at ashley@ashleyemmaauthor.com if you have questions, suggestions, or want to share your success story.

Here's to your work-at-home success!

Ashley

About the Author

Ashley Emma knew she wanted to be a novelist for as long as she can remember. She was home-schooled and was blessed with the opportunity to spend her time focusing on reading and writing. She began writing books for fun at a young age, completing her first novella at age 12 and writing her first novel at age 14, then publishing it at age 16.

She went on to write 8 more manuscripts before age 25 when she also became a multi-bestselling author.

She owns Fearless Publishing House where she helps other aspiring authors achieve their dreams of publishing their own books.

Ashley lives in Maine with her husband and children and plans on releasing several more books in the near future.

Visit her at ashleyemmaauthor.com or email her at:

ashley@ashleyemmaauthor.com. She loves to hear from her readers!

If you enjoyed this book, would you consider leaving a review? Reviews tremendously help authors because they help other customers decide whether or not they want to buy the book or not.

Here is the link: http://a.co/9zVadYc

Thank you!!

Looking for something new to read? Check out my other books!

All my books are available exclusively on Amazon

Coming soon:

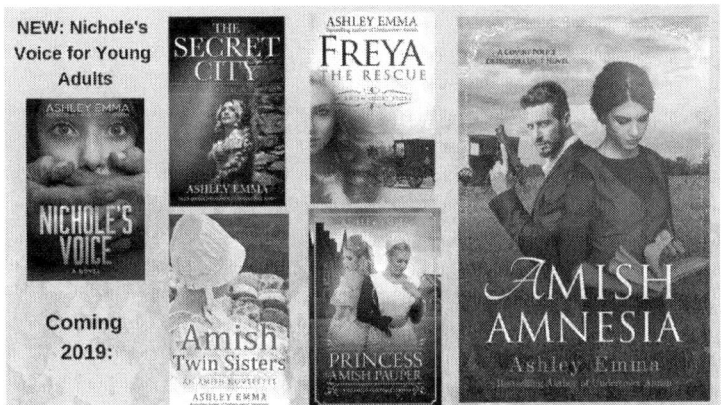

New release: AMISH UNDER FIRE

After Maria Mast's abusive ex-boyfriend is arrested for being involved in sex trafficking and modern-day slavery, she thinks that she and her son Carter are finally safe.
But the danger has only just begun. Someone begins stalking her, and they want blood and revenge.

Agent Derek Turner of Covert Police Detectives Unit is assigned as her bodyguard. When Maria returns home to her former Amish community in Unity, Maine, Derek goes with her as her undercover bodyguard, and tried to blend in with the other Amish men.

Maria's secretive eyes, painful past, and cautious demeanor intrigue him as the stalker closes in.

Just search for Ashley Emma on Amazon.com.

Have you always dreamed of becoming an author?

"...The list of places to promote your book along with the step-by-step publishing and marketing checklist is well worth the cost of this eBook."

---Nicole Cruz, www.nicolecruzproofreader.com

In *Fearless Author*, I will show you how I launched my own bestselling books.

Just search for Ashley Emma on Amazon.com

UNDERCOVER AMISH

Detective Olivia Mast would rather run through gunfire than return to her former Amish community in Unity, Maine, where she killed her abusive husband in self-defense.

Since the community will not pursue justice or answer questions from the police, Olivia begrudgingly dons her old prayer kapp and covertly investigates a murder there while protecting the man she dated as a teen: Isaac Troyer, a potential target. The handsome and quirky cabinet maker falls in love with her once again, unaware that she carries a 9mm under her skirt. After another murder, some deadly pranks and a kidnapping, Olivia realizes she needs Isaac's help most of

Just search for Ashley Emma on Amazon.com

Free eBook! FREYA: AN AMISH SHORT STORY (Book 1 in the Freya Series)

Click here to get my free book, Freya: an Amish Short Story!

After Freya Wilson accidentally hits an Amish man with her car in a storm, will she have the courage to tell his family the truth—especially after she meets his handsome brother?

Just search for Ashley Emma on Amazon.com or go to www.AshleyEmmaAuthor.com.

New release! FREYA: THE CONFESSION (Book 2 in the Freya Series)

Adam Lapp expected the woman who killed his brother accidentally with her car to be heartless and cruel. He never expected her to a timid, kind, and beautiful woman who is running for her life from a controlling ex who wants her dead.

When Freya Wilson asks him to take her to his family so she can tell them the truth, he agrees.

Will she find hope in the ashes, or just more darkness and sorrow?

Just search for Ashley Emma on Amazon.com or go to www.AshleyEmmaAuthor.com.

ASHLEY'S AMISH ADVENTURES: AN OUTSIDER LIVING WITH THE AMISH

Ever wondered what it would be like to live in an Amish community? Now you can find out in his true story for young adults and middle grade readers.

Just search for Ashley Emma on Amazon.com.

ASHLEY'S AMISH ADVENTURES: ATTENDING AN AMISH WEDDING

Ever wondered what it would be like to go inside an Amish home, make Amish friends, or go to an Amish wedding? Because of this journal's rare photos, you will literally get to see the places you are reading about as you read.

Just search for Ashley Emma on Amazon.com

An Excerpt from *Fearless Author*: Prepare, Publish, and Launch Your Own eBook

You know what I love most about self-publishing?

Anyone can do it, no matter how young or old you are, as long as you are determined enough and willing to learn.

You can do it if you're eight, eighteen, or eighty-five!

You can write about what you love—write what you are passionate about—without waiting for permission first. Or you can use a book to build your business by bringing in new leads or establishing yourself as an expert.

I wrote my first novel when I was only fourteen and self-published it when I was only sixteen. I self-published three more while I was still a teenager and started making passive income.

I wrote eight full-length manuscripts by the time I was twenty-five, and I became a multi-bestselling author at the same age.

If I can do it, you can do it.

Be fearless!

Are you ready to write your first book? Or maybe you have written a book but are not sure what to do with it. Maybe it's been rejected by publishers or agents and you're feeling discouraged.

There is no reason why you should have to wait for permission from an agent or publisher to be published.

In the past, self-publishing was considered by many to be a "last resort" for authors who weren't good enough to be accepted by traditional publishing house.

Not anymore.

In my opinion, self-publishing is the way to go.

No more asking for permission or changing your storylines when an agent asks you to. You can write whatever you want!

No more waiting months to snag an agent's attention and then wait even longer while they submit your work to publishers.

This entire process can take months or years.

With self-publishing, you can publish your books in only a few short weeks or months and keep a much higher percentage of your book royalties than you would with a publisher. Plus, you don't have to give an agent a percentage of your royalties.

The more eBooks you publish, the more you will make. Once you get the hang of it, it only becomes easier each time. Maybe you're not interested in making money and just want to publish a book that you are passionate about that you know will help people.

Maybe you want to write a book that will establish you as an authority figure and will drive leads to your business. This works great for doctors, chiropractors, coaches, consultants, realtors, etc.

Self-publishing will enable you to do that.

And if you start young like I did, imagine where you will be when you're in your twenties or thirties! But don't worry; if you're not a teenager anymore, now is still a fantastic time to get started, no matter what your age is.

However, it is not for the faint of heart if you want your book to be successful. This journey requires a massive amount of work and some investment upfront, but when done correctly, you will reap the profits of passive income on your eBook for years to come.

But with the help of this book—if you commit and do the work—you can be successful. It won't be easy, but it will be rewarding!

I tried the traditional publishing route. When I finally did find an agent, one of the best in the Christian publishing industry, she held on to my work for a full eighteen months without doing anything with it. I can't believe how much time was wasted during those months. I could have been making money from self-publishing.

I finally realized I was getting nowhere and decided to self-publish when I learned how much quicker the process is! Once I talked to Stacy Claflin, a USA Today Bestselling Author and an indie author, I decided I wanted to follow in her footsteps.

I'm an extremely ambitious and motivated person, and I hated waiting around for someone to give me permission to move forward. She publishes several books a year—many more than she would be if she were traditionally published.

I am so glad I chose this path. Harlequin's Christian line rejected *Undercover Amish* twice and I have probably already made more money from it than I would have if I had published with them.

I've heard Dr. Seuss was rejected by over two dozen publishers before he was finally published. Just imagine how many publishers might reject you and how long that process would take. Often publishers will reject manuscripts because it is not exactly what they are looking for. It doesn't always mean your book isn't well written. They usually want authors who already have their own audience—a massive email list, a huge Twitter or Facebook following, etc.

I won't lie, self-publishing is a ton of work. You can't read this book and expect great things to happen without putting in the work. Book launches are tough, and you are responsible for EVERYTHING. There are so many steps involved, as you will see below. But, in my opinion, the reward is so much greater because you have complete control over your work, you can make more money, publish more books in less time, and do it the way you want to do it.

This guide describes the steps I take for preparing, publishing, marketing, and launching my books. There's no fluff, just valuable information and links, so you can implement these strategies and get results quickly.

There are many methods authors use, and it's hard to tell what will work and what won't until you try.

I invested hundreds of dollars in training and saw tremendous success with my first book. I'm going to share the basics of my process with you. Hopefully, you can follow similar steps and see positive results. But just because this method worked for me doesn't mean it will work for you, especially if you don't put in the time and work that it will involve. I can't make any guarantees because I don't know if you will actually apply these strategies or not. Also, there are many variables involved, such as how well written your book is, the genre, and how popular that genre is, etc.

This book will cover the basic steps I took for building my email list. It describes my beta reading process, how I get editorial reviews and how to use them, and how I deal with bad reviews (most authors get them!). It also covers how I use permafree books to build my audience, and how I compare self-publishing to traditional and vanity publishing.

This book concludes with a book launch checklist for your convenience and a list of links of resources I mention throughout the book. As you read and take in this information, remember that everything will be summarized at the end in a concise checklist, so you don't need to take notes, unless you want to.

There is also the exact beta reading questionnaire I send to my beta readers and a list of the experts I hire such as cover designers.

If you're new to the wonderful world of self-publishing, this eBook may seem overwhelming to you! That's okay. I was overwhelmed when I first began as well.

Take your time going through this book and the process of publishing. If you need help, feel free to reach out to me. If you do follow these steps with your book launch, I'd love to know your results. Please email me at ashley@ashleyemmaauthor.com and tell me how it went!

My Launch Statistics

My book launch for my first book *Undercover Amish* went WAY better than I thought it would. Here are some of my statistics:

- 8,424 downloads in 3.5 days!

- 50+ reviews in the first week with a 5-star average (and the reviews keep rolling in)

- #1 in two categories: biblical, and religious and inspirational mystery

- Reached #53 in Top 100 Free eBooks list

- *Undercover Amish* is a #1 Amazon bestseller!

The Most Important Lessons I Learned

- **I invested time and money in training, and it really paid off.** I used to think you could just upload a book onto Amazon and people would magically find it and buy it. Now I know the right way to launch and market a book to bring in sales.

- **Launching my book over a holiday gave me more downloads.** The launch of *Undercover Amish* began on a Sunday and ended the following Wednesday afternoon. Looking back, that promotion was probably too long and should have been two and a half days. However, I think that the fact that Monday was a holiday (Labor Day) helped tremendously because I had the most downloads that day by far!

- **Start building your email list long before you plan on launching your book.** Ideally, you will want at least 100 people on your list because you will be asking them to be on your launch team, and only a fraction of them will follow through and review your book.

- **Give yourself plenty of time to launch your book.** Don't rush through it like I did when I set my launch date too early. I wanted to start making money as soon as possible, but then I rushed the process. Your launch date is the date you pick to start promoting your book after you upload and publish it on Amazon. I recommend choosing this date AFTER your book is completely ready to publish.

You may choose it beforehand if you think it will help you not procrastinate. If you do this, make sure you give yourself plenty of time and have the time to do all the work involved. However, I recommend waiting to set your launch date until the book has been beta read, edited, and published, especially for your first book.

***

If you enjoyed this excerpt, just search for Ashley Emma on Amazon.com.

Made in the USA
Monee, IL
21 November 2019